CHRIS
DIOR

CHRISTIAN DIOR

Diana de Marly

B.T. Batsford Ltd London

First published 1990
© Diana de Marly 1990
ISBN 0 7134 6453 4

Filmset by Lasertext Ltd., Manchester

and printed in Great Britain by
The Bath Press, Bath

for the publishers
B.T. Batsford Ltd,
4 Fitzhardinge Street,
London W1H 0AH

Frontispiece
**A Dior New Look cocktail dress,
Cecil Beaton, 1947.**

Fashion Designers is a new series which looks at
the work of the most important designers, from the
great couturiers of the past to the designers who
are making the headlines today. Each book
provides a concise assessment of the work of the
designer with reference to their influence on the
development of fashion, design procedures and
commercial attitudes. Supported by unusual black
and white and colour illustrations and helpful
appendices documenting collections worldwide, the
series will interest students, designers and fashion
followers alike

T

CONTENTS

LIST OF ILLUSTRATIONS

LIST OF COLOUR PLATES

(between pages 48 and 49)

ACKNOWLEDGEMENTS

To Zika Ascher for his memories of Dior: to Avril Lansdell and Peter Hope Lumley for their memories of 1947; to Mrs L. Poole, Archivist of the John Lewis Partnership. And to the following museum staff who have sent the details of their Dior holdings: Susan Shifrin, Boston Museum of Fine Arts; Otto Charles Thieme, Cincinnati Art Museum; Monica Brown, Philadelphia Museum of Art; Penny Byrde, Bath Museum of Costume; Richard Robson, Castle Howard Costume Galleries; Valerie D. Mendes, Victoria and Albert Museum, London; Elizabeth Jachimowicz, Chicago Historical Society.

1

TOWARDS COUTURE

Christian Dior was born in Normandy on 21 January 1905, at the small seaside resort of Granville, overlooking the Gulf of St Malo. He was the second of five children and had two brothers and two sisters. His father, Alexandre Louis Maurice Dior, was a chemical fertilizer manufacturer and comfortably off. As a little boy Dior was dressed in the English fashion for sailor suits, which shows that his parents were Anglophiles, following the Anglo–French *entente cordiale* of 1904. The happy seaside childhood ended in 1910 when the family moved to Paris, although they still returned to Granville for holidays. The children had a governess Madeleine Lefebvre, but for his secondary education, 1916–23, Dior was sent to the school at Gerson. His interest in clothes

1 *Sir John Lavery RA, Hazel in Black and Gold, 1916, from the collection at the Laing Art Gallery Newcastle-upon Tyne. The fashions of Dior's childhood would inspire the New Look when he was an adult. He revived the sloping shoulder line and the full skirts with the hemline skimming the ankle in 1947 (Reproduced by permission of Tyne and Wear Museums Service).*

first showed itself in his teens, when he dressed up as King Neptune at a fancy dress party at Granville Casino, and indeed his love of dressing-up continued all through his life. He wanted to become an architect but the family were determined that he should aim for the diplomatic corps, and paid for him to attend the Ecole des Sciences Politiques over 1923–6, where he obtained his B.Sc. While studying political science his real interest was the arts, and he frequented circles where he met people from the art world. In 1927 he had to serve his national service, after which he told his father that he wanted to run a gallery for modern art. Monsieur Dior was shocked but he provided the money, on condition that the family name did not appear over the door. Thus it was Dior's collaborator in the project, Jacques Bonjean, whose name was installed over the Galerie Jacques Bonjean, 34 rue La Boetie, Paris in 1928. To his parents, both born in the nineteenth century, any involvement with avant-garde art was suspect, but Dior and Bonjean exhibited the pioneers of the period, Braque, de Chirico, Dufy, Marie Laurencin, Maurice Utrillo, Léger, and Picasso.

In 1931 Madame Dior died: Dior was always to remember her as a very elegant lady. To recover from the loss Dior seized the opportunity to join a party of architects on a visit to the USSR, where Dior was fascinated by the Russo–Byzantine churches. On his return he found that the impact of the Great Depression had reached his father who was ruined, so the gallery had to be sold in 1932. Dior helped at the gallery of Pierre Collé who specialized in surrealists like Salvador Dali, but Dior led a very hand to mouth existence over the next two years. Jean Ozenne was one artist who helped by teaching Dior fashion drawing, and Max Kenna showed him how to use colour. Dior was able to sell some hat designs to Agnès in 1933. In 1934 he developed tuberculosis. His friends financed his convalescence, spent partly on the Balearic Islands where he learnt tapestry weaving. In 1935 he went to live with Jean Ozenne, and Max Kenna told him to sell his designs to the couture houses, so from September 1935 to 1938 this became the basis of Dior's life, designing clothes and hats, and taking them to couturiers. He made regular sales to Agnès, Patou, Schiaparelli, Nina Ricci, Maggy Rouf, Piguet, Molyneux, Worth, Paquin, Balenciaga, and many lesser houses. In 1936 his sketches first appeared in *Le Figaro*, where they featured until 1938. By 1937 he was earning enough to move into his own apartment at 10 rue

2 Christian Dior, 'From Goya to Winterhalter: the Parade of Styles', Le Figaro, 2 June 1938. Dior's drawing was one of the ways he earned his living before he entered couture. It shows that past fashions were the principal inspiration for his designs, reusing Empire waists seen in Goya, crinolines from Winterhalter, paniers after Chardin and Velasquez and the cuirass look after Manet. From the styles of his own lifetime he recycled the 1920s as the H Line. The accompanying text advocates that readers of the paper's women's pages should try out the styles illustrated (Photograph courtesy of Le Figaro).

DU «FIGARO»

2 JUIN 1938

DE GOYA A WINTER HALTER

YLES

Manet
l'Expo-
ardin »,
inspira-
s d'au-
contre
ude à
elques
es en-
oman-

VELASQUEZ

EXPOSITION ANGLAISE

CHARDIN

EUSE ESPAGNOLE

Chacune de ces silhouettes est charmante en soi ; certaines même ne souffrent point d'être juxtaposées. On conçoit que l'une, aussi bien que l'autre, soit digne de tenter une femme qui, consultant son miroir, chez elle, se réjouira à bon droit de son élégance pittoresque et sans fadeur. Le rapprochement, un peu arbitraire, que nous avons réalisé ici de toutes ces silhouettes nous montre cependant qu'il est peut-être temps de restreindre le choix des styles et de revenir à plus d'unité.

+...DIOR

WINTER HALTER

Royale in Paris, but he knew nothing of the construction of clothes, so another friend helped: the fashion designer Georges Geoffroy introduced Dior to the couturier Robert Piguet, who engaged him as a modeller in 1938. He had crossed the threshold into haute couture.

The modeller or *modeliste* was responsible for designing the creations. If approved by the studio of designers a design would be handed over to a work-room to be made up as the *toile*, a trial dress in cheap fabrics like calico or linen, to see how well the design worked, and what problems it might create over construction. As a would-be architect the structure of clothes fascinated Dior, so he applied himself to this discipline with great willingness. As he told *Cue* magazine in 1947:

> *When I decided to become a couturier I learned in every way what I had to do. It is a job you cannot improvise. Particularly in France where so many people know how to make dresses, you cannot fool [them].*[1]

Dior designed three collections while at Piguet's, and the most famous dress he created then was the *Café Anglais* where he showed a full short skirt for day.

During this brief spell in the house, as war loomed, Dior designed the costumes for two productions in which the actress Odette Joyeux appeared, Jean Planchon's *Captain Smith* at the Théâtre des Mathurins in December 1939, and Sheridan's *School for Scandal* which was staged as *L'Ecole de la Médisance* also at the Théâtre des Mathurins in February 1940. Dior dressed both productions in the crinolines of the Second Empire, and he would revive crinolines and bustles as a fashion designer, for he greatly admired the period when Charles Frederick Worth dressed the empresses of France, Austria and Russia.

In August 1939 Dior received his call-up papers. France was mobilizing her reserves

although war was not declared officially until the September. Dior was a soldier *première classe* in the troops at Génie. The first months saw little military activity on the western front, for Germany and her ally the Soviet Union were busy invading Poland and Finland. It was 1940 before Hitler turned his attention towards the Channel. His armies swept through neutral Belgium and Holland over 10–16 May, and on 14 June 1940 Paris was occupied. The French First Army surrendered on 1 June, and thereafter opposition collapsed. An armistice was signed on 25 June, and it left the Germans in control of two-thirds of French territory. The French government withdrew to Vichy. Her horse-drawn artillery was outflanked by Germany's armoured divisions. Dior was demobbed, as all French forces were in a state of confusion. He could not return to Piguet in occupied Paris, as he had engaged another designer Castillo, so Dior went to join his father and sister who were running a farm in Provence at Callian. Dior became a market gardener growing vegetables. He contacted *Le Figaro* and did some more illustrations for it that year. Plants were going to have a big impact on his future designs.

Dior spent about 18 months working as a market gardener, until in December 1941 he received an invitation to join Lucien Lelong's couture house back in Paris. Lelong was President of the Chambre Syndicale de la Haute Couture, and had been busy with negotiations with the Germans in an attempt to save French couture. In 1940 he had asked Captain Molyneux, the most famous British couturier in Paris, what the industry ought to do, and Molyneux had placed his branch at Biarritz at his disposal; thus Lelong, Schiaparelli and Molyneux had all set out for the south. But on the capitulation of France it was no longer safe for British passport holders to remain in the country, so Molyneux escaped to London, and

3 **Odette Joyeux in** Lettres d'amour, **1943, by Claude Autant Lara. Odette Joyeux wore Dior's crinolines on the stage, so when she began to appear in the costume dramas which the Nazi censors permitted, she took Dior with her. Films set in the Second Empire when Worth was the first grand couturier, gave Dior the opportunity to recreate dozens of vast dresses. The fact that the frills have been painted on to the fabric suggests an economic touch (National Film Archive London).**

Schiaparelli to the USA. Lelong had decided to return to Paris, to deal with the devil directly.

The Germans had seized all the documents relating to couture exports, and informed Lelong that they were going to move the industry to Berlin and Vienna. Lelong pleaded against this, for dividing the industry and transporting it would be both detrimental and impractical. Couture was not simply a group of fashion houses, but a network of sub-contractors and suppliers who made all the hats, the gloves, the stockings, the corsets, the shoes, the handbags, the jewellery, the buckles, the belts, and the buttons. There were the embroiderers, the make-up artists, and the hairdressers, in addition to all the representatives of the textile companies. One could not recreate such a complex entity in two other cities. Eventually the Germans relented, and Paris

couture was allowed to remain by the Seine. Lelong had started to recruit more staff, which was how Dior found himself invited to join Lelong's design studio, alongside Pierre Balmain. Balmain had trained under Molyneux in 1934 to 1939, and when Dior took his apartment in the rue Royale in 1937 he was only just across the road from Maison Molyneux at number five. Dior had visited that shrine of discreet elegance and sophisticated restraint, where the walls were lined with pearl grey satin, when he was selling his drawings. Now he had a design companion who could tell him exactly how matters were conducted at that eminent establishment. Molyneux himself was now busy in London, coping with a flood of orders from American stores who had all switched their requests for licensed copying from occupied Paris to London.

The Germans introduced clothes rationing for the masses, but couture was excluded, so that it could supply German officers' wives. The occupation government reduced the number of couture houses to 20, and restricted the amount of fabric produced, so the collections had to be smaller, with only about 100 models, but Lelong encouraged everyone to keep going as best they could under the restrictions, in order to keep the industry ticking over as they all prayed for Liberation. Paris was lucky in that she was not subjected to heavy air raids for she possessed no heavy industry or docks, unlike London, so the couture houses led a relatively charmed existence when Dior rejoined them.

Dior was a great believer in luck, and never took an important decision without consulting fortune tellers. One prophesy he liked to recall all his life had been made in 1919. He had gone to a charity bazaar in aid of soldiers, dressed up as a gipsy, and a fortune teller had read his lines.[2] She forecast that Dior would find himself without money, but women were very beneficial where he was concerned, and they would cause him to have a great success. Dior liked to believe this forecast, but the facts were rather different. His period of greatest poverty was in the early 1930s, when it was his male friends who helped, and taught him to build a new career through his drawing. Another male friend introduced him to Piguet, so his entry into couture did not involve a single woman.

The German censors restricted the

French film industry to non-political subjects, and costume dramas were encouraged. This was to benefit Dior, for during the occupation he costumed several historical films. This is where the first woman could be seen to be influential, but Dior was no longer poor but in a steady job. The actress Odette Joyeux, whom Dior had dressed on the stage, began to make a regular appearance in these costume films, and it was most likely she who recommended Dior to the film companies. Roland Tual's *Le Lit à Colonnes* of 1942 was set in the 1860s and 1870s so Dior was called upon to recreate crinolines and bustles to his heart's content. In 1943 Claude Autant-Lara's *Lettres d'Amour* again featured Odette Joyeux in Dior's crinolines after Worth, and in 1944 he had the opportunity to recreate eighteenth-century paniers for Jean Paulin's *Echec au Roi*. As Dior was fascinated by structure, this was a period of charmed opportunity to visit museum archives and study the construction of eighteenth- and nineteenth-century clothes, prior to recreating them for the cinema. It is hardly surprising that crinolines, paniers, and bustle effects would all appear later in his fashions. At Lelong's Dior showed the hobble skirt, shades of Poiret, and rounded draperies after Worth, for he was clearly a believer in recycling old styles.

Liberation came in 1944. After an elaborate scheme to fool the Germans that the Allies were intending to invade Calais, on D-Day, 6 June, they actually landed in Dior's native Normandy. The breakthrough

4 *Yvonne Printemps in* Valse de Paris, *1947, by Marcel Achard. This film was a real tribute to Worth and the Second Empire. Printemps played the operetta star Hortense Schneider who was dressed by Worth both on and off the stage. Worth was Dior's favourite predecessor, and this spangled, multi-frilled skirt and crinoline attempts to recall the glitter of the 1860s (National Film Archive London).*

came at the end of July when Avranches was liberated, and the Allies raced for Paris, which was freed on 25 August 1944. The war was not over until 1945, but for the Parisians life began slowly to return to normal, although shortages continued for years. It was not until hostilities were over that haute couture could even begin to consider a new line for peacetime, and the indications that several minds were trying to find a new silhouette emerged in 1946. The square shouldered look which Schiaparelli had introduced in 1933, had become a uniform, so in 1946 a more feminine shape began to appear. In the spring Molyneux showed a checked dress with padded hips although it still had square shoulders. *Harper's Bazaar* in April 1946 greeted the London collections, 'Softer, rounder runs the London line. You have hips. You have a waist. You have a bosom. You have round, natural shoulders.' The same magazine reported the Paris autumn collections with the news, 'Skirts definitely longer, averaging 3 to 5 inches below the knee.' The hour glass figure was the new ideal, as in Balenciaga's wasp waisted suits, which had long jackets padded over the hips. Coats with Magyar sleeves had sloping shoulders, the first sign of a major difference in the silhouette emerging.[3]

The textile designers Lida and Zika Ascher were in Paris for the autumn collections 1946. Czech refugees, they had set up in London in 1942 where Captain Molyneux gave them the *entrée* into couture by agreeing to use their abstract patterns on his summer frocks. The first Paris couturier to use their screen-printed silks was Pierre Balmain, Molyneux's ex-pupil, who left Lelong to open his own house in autumn 1944. The Aschers went to Lelong's to see the collections, and among the square shouldered models there was a group by Dior with sloping shoulders. They looked strange but different so Lida bought one in black. When it came to the fitting she had some qualms, for it was so unlike the clothes she was used to. But it was too late to cancel the order, and Lida wore the dress next time they visited Pierre Balmain. 'Oh, c'est raté!' Balmain exclaimed. 'That is a failure. Leave it with me and I shall improve it.' He promptly added lots of coloured drapery around the waist. Later Lida regretted that the dress had been altered.[4] It was one of several experiments towards a new line, with padded hips, wasp waists, longer skirts and sloping shoulders, so Dior was participating in a movement, and was not, as history since has tended to think, the sole originator. London and Paris were looking for a change in the silhouette, and New York too showed some drooping hemlines so the mood was fully established in 1946. What was needed now was someone to pull all the ideas together, and give the trend a name and an identity, and who clearly knew what the new post-war woman should look like. The person who identified the line was Dior.

2

A NEW HOUSE, A NEW LINE

One day in 1946, probably in the summer, Dior was walking through the Paris streets when he met an old childhood friend, whom he used to play with on the beach at Granville. He did not say who the friend was, but he was now a director of the dressmakers Philippe et Gaston, which had been founded in 1925. The firm was having a difficult time, and as the friend had heard that Dior was in design nowadays, could he suggest a designer in a million who could give the firm new life? Dior could not off hand, but he went to inspect the business and found it full of old established staff, very set in their ways, who would prove an obstacle to any new ideas. Philippe et Gaston was owned by the cotton magnate Marcel Boussac, so very nervously Dior went to see him. Boussac was the son of a successful draper who had left him £70,000 to set up his own business in 1909. Rejected for military service on health grounds, Boussac began to supply the French Army with cotton clothing and webbing during the First World War. When the war ended he bought up huge amounts of military surplus cloth in Britain and France and became a cheap clothing manufacturer, producing dresses, shirts, pyjamas, and overalls. By the 1920s he was a millionaire, and started to appear at race meetings in his grey top hat, and acquired his own stud farm at Jardy. During the Depression Boussac bought up several bankrupt firms with cotton mills in the Vosges, and so built himself up into France's biggest cotton spinner and weaver. He did well because of France's protective laws against foreign textiles, and the captive market of the French colonies.

Dior was usually too shy and nervous to confront anybody, but when he met the emperor of cotton, he found himself declaring that Philippe et Gaston was a hopeless case. He did not want to work for another house. He wanted his own firm where he could put forward new ideas unsupervised by Lelong. It was time for fashion to change, and break out of the square silhouette of the war, with its short skirts. He liked long skirts, full skirts, crinolines, lots of petticoats like in his childhood, skirts which open out like flowers in bloom. Boussac pricked up his ears at this. Fuller skirts meant more fabric, so the textile industry would be given the

opportunity to start to increase production if Dior could promise to make larger skirts fashionable. He put the proposal to his board, and they agreed. Boussac offered Dior 10 million francs to start his own business. At this Dior panicked, never having organized a company before, so he rushed to see his fortune teller Madame Delahaye. She told him to accept the challenge. Appreciating Dior's lack of business flair, Boussac sent him a business manager who was created director general, Jacques Rouët. The new company was registered on 8 October 1946, and recruited 85 staff with three workrooms, one of tailors and two of seamstresses. Dior would be the artistic director responsible for the creations, Rouët would watch the money. This sensible arrangement was unique in couture, for other houses had to open and struggle to make money before they could engage business managers, but Rouët started work at Maison Dior, 30 avenue Montaigne, Paris 8ᵉ on day one.

Dior resigned from Lelong on 16 December 1946, and no doubt he reflected that his old design partner Pierre Balmain had had his own house for two years now. Dior was now going solo at 41, and he would not have done so without Boussac. The modest mansion of five floors, but only three windows wide, that was Maison Dior was in the smart arrondissement between the Champs Elysées and the Seine. It was further west than Worth's rue de la Paix or the Boulevard Saint Honoré, but not too distant for taxi drivers to object. Victor Grandpierre did the décor and Christian Bérard designed the boutique for

5 **Captain Molyneux, 'Day dress with fuller hips',** Harper's Bazaar, **March 1946.** One of the many 'first steps' toward the New Look, which took place in 1946, when skirts went below the knee, and both Molyneux and Balenciaga started introducing padded hips. Dior's main contribution was to discard square shoulders.

accessories. Dior decided he wanted grey interiors, like Molyneux, not that Molyneux had originated the idea, for his teacher Lucile had had grey salons in her houses in London, Paris, New York and Chicago before the First World War. Dior opted for shades of dark and light grey outlined with white, to create a quiet, discreet ambience that would not challenge the clothes, in the British manner. He did not go so far as to copy Molyneux by having grey uniforms for the staff, but here kept to the French tradition of black dresses on the leading ladies, with white overalls in the workrooms. He recruited firstly Raymonde Zehnacker, the storekeeper at Lelong's who had looked after him while in that house, and appointed her to run the studio. Marguerite Carré, after 18 years at Patou, came to direct the workrooms, and would be the technician responsible for converting Dior's drawings into clothes. From Molyneux he begged his stylist Mitzah Bricard, who had been there in the 1930s when Balmain remembered her way of dressing with low necklines filled with pearls, and she was a hat designer. She agreed to transfer to the new house.

Most of the staff came by word of mouth, for all couture was buzzing with the news that Boussac was backing Dior. The Aschers heard the rumours in autumn 1946 and went and sold Dior some silks for his first presentation. He also ordered their silk headscarves which had designs by Henry Moore, Graham Sutherland and many other contemporary artists, to be sold in the new boutique. Seven mannequins were taken on to model the clothes, as the new house worked overtime to prepare the first collection for 12 February 1947.

Dior wrote of his intentions 'We came from an epoch of war and uniforms, with women like soldiers with boxers' shoulders. I designed flower women, soft shoulders, full busts, waists as narrow as lianas, and skirts as corollas.'[1] These were

both botanical terms, showing Dior's use of nature as a source for ideas, the liana being the creeper in tropical forests, and the corolla the whorl of a leaf or petal before it opens out. Dior wanted to express this opening out quality in skirts, from the tight narrow skirts of the early 1940s, into a wider, unfolding, blooming sort of skirt. Moreover he said that as a frustrated architect, he wanted his clothes to be constructed, and moulded on to the body. He lined his dresses with cambric and taffeta to give them more body, and he used whalebones to curve and shape the garments. He intended to reshape women. He emphasised the width of the hips, restricted the waist, and gave the bust more prominence. He told his slim model girls to start wearing falsies to produce the rounder bustline he wanted. This led to one mishap. During the strain of preparing for the first show, his English model fainted. Dior grabbed her, but the girl slid to the ground leaving him with a pair of falsies in his hands, as she had slipped out of them.

Harper's Bazaar greeted his first collection as 'a sensational success'. *Elle* declared that the name which shone was Dior. He launched two new lines, the Corolla and the Figure of Eight, and in his programme notes wrote that the first was a dancing line, dressed up with petticoats, with a moulded bust and narrow waist, and the second was a very shaped and clear cut line, with the bust underlined, the waist narrow, and the hips accentuated. He actually used the term excavated to describe the waist – thinking of women as building sites.

In *Elle* Chamine wrote that the Corolla was a bustline which then opened out into a supple bell composed of regular or irregular pleats, suggestive of the dance, and youthful paces. Carmel Snow dubbed the new line the New Look, and by 1948 all the magazines were using the term, even the French as 'le New Look'.

Harper's reported:

> *Dior affects mild surprise at the furore that has greeted his designs, for he considers them, as befits an introductory collection, to be simple and conservative. But to the fashion world, his long billowing skirts, high small waists, and narrow shoulders, are both revolutionary and immensely chic.*[2]

The magazine made the point that the difference between Balenciaga's long padded jackets and Dior's, was that Dior's were structured to stand out from the body. They did not depend on the padding for their shape, they were curved in construction, so that the basques were rounded even when off the wearer. Dior had designed enough crinolines to know how to achieve an architectural effect. What took everyone's breath away was the sheer opulence of the collections. Ordinary clothes were still rationed, but here was Dior employing lavish amounts of fabric, and the most luxurious stuffs like silk and satin, in a world of shortages. It was scandalous said many, especially the British, and in the USA an anti-Dior club was founded, the Little Below the Knee Club, where the women members objected to longer skirts, and chopped off the New Look when it appeared in the shops. *Elle* stated that Dior's hems were 36 cms from the floor, that is just over 14 inches. That was not dramatically different from the hems of autumn 1946, when Balenciaga had them five inches below the knee. But there was more hemline on a Dior skirt.

*6 Le Bar, **the first Dior model in his first collection, February 1947. The white shantung jacket has the shoulder line of 1916 (see fig. 1), and is fitted to the bust, with sculpted basques which stand out from the body. The skirt was of deeply-pleated black cloth. In the house it was presented with a black hat (Musée des Arts de la Mode, Paris).***

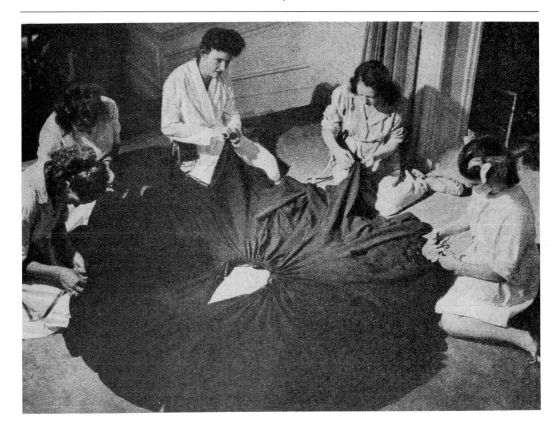

They were voluminous, so their impact was much greater.

Dior had called his look conservative, and it was, if one looked back to his childhood and the styles of the First World War. That was the last time when lots of petticoats had been worn, when fashion suddenly took notice of what the troops at the front were demanding, and created a very feminine style, with sloping shoulders, small waists, and full skirts, in complete contrast to the narrow line of fashion's principal ideal before and after that war. But 33 years is a long time in most people's memories, so to them Dior's line was the New Look, not the recreation of the styles his mother had worn. Orders flooded in and Maison Dior had to open two additional workrooms. The principal colours were black, grey, marine blue and raw silk. The first outfit in the first collection was *Bar*, a jacket in natural

7 Seamstresses working on one of Dior's enormous skirts, Savitry and Geiger, Picture Post, 27 September 1947. For ordinary women rationing meant that the New Look was impossible to achieve and it was 1948 before the clothing industry could even attempt to copy the style. This example from an afternoon dress required nearly 50 yards of material, and horrified the press (British Library).

shantung silk with a tailored collar and rounded basques, with a pleated skirt of black wool. The dress for afternoons *Corolla* bore the name of the collection as a whole and was of black wool, fastened down the front of the bodice with five large buttons from a collarless neckline. The skirt had a plain panel in centre front, but otherwise was densely pleated, over swelling petticoats. The same type of skirt appeared on *Chérie* in marine-blue silk taffeta, with the plain panel in front and lots of pleats at the sides, but a gather ran through the pleats at hip level. The bodice

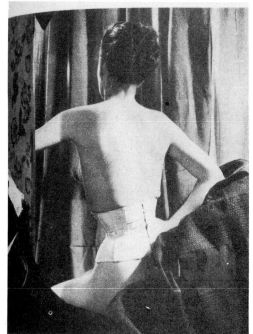

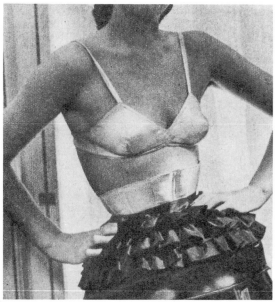

*9 **A New Look coat, Seeberger Frères, February 1947.** The hips are built out like paniers, and require panels to be inserted under the pockets. The bodice and sleeves are tightly fitted. On his first collection the hemline was just below the knee, as it was for other couturiers. It was the second collection which saw the sensational drop in hemlines (Bibliothèque Nationale Paris).*

was cut without sleeves. There were some slender skirts, for example, the tailored suit *Passe-Partout* in marine-blue crepe wool, which had no collar, pockets on the chest and on the basques, and a narrow skirt that offered an alternative to so many pleated ones. The sleeves were cuffed, and the jacket only buttoned as far as the waist. Pleats also dominated the evening gowns, and the model *Soirée* had two tiers of pleated skirts one above the other, in marine-blue taffeta. Jungle-print muslins were a common feature for after dark, notably in the long gown *Africain* which had a panther print employed on the gown and a floating panel from the right waist. The film star Rita Hayworth visited the presentation and bought the evening gown *Soirée* to wear at the gala of her latest film *Gilda*, and the black suit *Pompom*, which had a narrow skirt and highly excavated waistline, with the jacket and hemline trimmed with pompoms. The price of the suit *Passe-Partout* was 30,000 francs. In his programme notes Dior said that he had deliberately avoided hobble skirts, asymmetry, and the over-employment of drapery, which suggests he now found his styles at Lelong too fussy to express his new line.

The New Look fully expressed the type of woman which most governments in the West were looking for. Yes, women had done a magnificent job during the war building warships and bombers, but would they kindly go back to the kitchen and let the demobbed soldiers have the factory posts. From being all-capable, women were now told to become decorative

stereotypes, and semi consciously Dior was co-operating in this sort of propaganda. His flower-woman was intended to replace the big-shouldered image that the war had encouraged.

Once the collection was launched Dior had to set about matching its success for his autumn collections in August. His policy was to launch two new lines a season, that is four new lines a year, which he continued until 1951, when he must have found the demands on his creative imagination too much, and thereafter reduced the new lines to about two. Even so, over the ten years of his career 1947–57, he introduced 30 new lines, so it is hardly surprising that the beat generation turned its back on such excess.

The new lines for autumn were Corolla again, and the Back of Paris where bustle effects were employed. Boussac probably encouraged Dior to put even more fabric into his skirts, for this second collection had reporters complaining about the amounts. *Harper's Bazaar* recorded skirts 25 yards (23 metres) round the hem. *Elle*

10 *An afternoon dress, Seeberger Frères, February 1947. The tight bodice is here softened by a draped neckline. The skirt is pleated from the hips, and it was this pleating of huge amounts of fabric which stunned a world of shortages (Bibliothèque Nationale Paris).*

called them parachute skirts, and cited the black two piece *Diorama* which had 20 metres ($21\frac{7}{8}$ yards) of cloth in it, an afternoon outfit. Allowing one metre for the bodice which had short sleeves, a V neck, and was fastened by tiny buttons to the waist, then 19 metres ($20\frac{3}{4}$ yards) had gone into the skirt which was pleated and repleated over itself, to form very deep folds. *Harper's* observed that the model girls had learned how to manage such skirts for this presentation, and they danced into the salon, spinning round, and turning, so that the huge skirts opened out and swung like enormous full blown flowers. Dior said as much in his programme notes: 'The collection affirms the natural graces of Woman. Woman the stem, Woman the Flower. The Corolla silhouette opens into a tulip, which is expressed most powerfully in the dress *Diorama*.' He also dropped the hemline to the ankle on some coats and dresses, very much in the look of 1916, he said 'to return to the legs all their mystery'. Thus he named the ankle-skimming coat *Mystère*, which was in black cloth bordered at the collar and the centre front of the skirt with pleated taffeta in eucalyptus green. The afternoon dress *Aladin* kept this magical mystery association in champagne coloured satin. The bodice was collarless with short sleeves decked with knots, and the waist was squeezed into a black patent leather belt. Not all the collection was so long, for *Bonbon*, a black woollen shirtwaister with a pleated skirt only came to below the

11 *The coat* Mystère, *Eric, British* Vogue, *Autumn—Winter 1947. Black cloth, with pleated eucalyptus green taffeta collar, matching the pleated dress beneath. The hemline plunges to just above the ankle. This second collection was attended by more American buyers, and Marshall Fields store, Chicago, bought a copy of this coat which is now in the Metropolitan Museum New York. (Condé Nast Publications).*

12 *A cocktail dress, Seeberger Frères, September 1947. On some models the hemline was near the ankle, as Dior looked back to the lengths of 1916, when he was aged 11. The bodice is boned, and the skirt has two squared corners at the waist to achieve width (Bibliothèque Nationale Paris).*

useful to discard. A range of satin evening gowns in bright colours were intended to be worn under fur coats. The Back of Paris line consisting of drapery and gathers at the back of skirts to achieve a bustle effect, and large bows over the backside, was founded mostly on evening clothes, with *Scarabée* as its examplar in a narrow skirt gathered behind. Many of the gowns Dior said were endeavouring to undress dress, by which he probably meant that they were intended to appear more casual.

The collection was strongly criticized in *Picture Post* by Marjorie Becket under the headline 'Paris Forgets this is 1947'. The luxury in particular she found unforgivable.

> *Straight from the indolent and wealthy years before the 1914 war come this year's much discussed Paris fashions. They are launched upon a world which has not the material to copy them, and whose women have neither the money to buy, the leisure to copy, nor in some designs even the strength to support, these masses of elaborate material . . . We are back to the days when fashion was the prerogative of the leisured wealthy woman, and not the everyday concern of typist, saleswoman or housewife.*[3]

Dior's use of corsets and horsehair petticoats was grossly impractical for modern working women, she argued. Skirts with 20, 30 even 50 yards (46 metres) of material crammed in could not be worn in offices or shops, and no British woman's clothing coupons could allow so much fabric in a dress. The cost was astounding, £80 for a day dress, £250 for an evening gown, decorated with embroidery or fur. These clothes were a scandal. She wrote from a Britain which had seen fuel cuts in February 1947, a reduction in the soap ration, and which had almost two million people unemployed. A special Parliament of Women condemned the low quality of goods in the shops, and the rising prices. It was a familiar story, Britain was importing

calves, and it was also available in pink.

There was much more colour in this second collection. Black and grey, the standards, were joined by red, scarlet, satanic red, greens from leaf to lichen, and a range of pinks. Having made day dresses longer, Dior showed some evening gowns with shorter hems, and said 'the dancing pace created by lifting the fabric gives the bottom of skirts a marked irregularity.' He had avoided asymmetry in his first collection, but here it was back again in his second, so presumably he found it too more than she sold, so by the September the Tory press was blaming the Labour government for a financial crisis. The one happy note was a royal wedding in Westminster Abbey when the heir to the throne Princess Elizabeth married Lt. Philip Mountbatten R.N. on 20 November. The most common feeling in the country was 'Where are the fruits of Victory? We won the war, didn't we?' Hardly any women watching the royal wedding procession were wearing the New Look, for as Majorie Becket had stressed they did not have the clothing coupons or the money to enable them to undertake such a major alteration to their wardrobes. Moreover the industry did not have the material to enable it to embark on a sudden mass production of longer skirts. The only large quantities in stock were of army khaki and parachute nylon, not the sort of fabrics Dior worked with. It was his flaunting of opulence and luxury in a world of shortages and bombed cities which made the British so angry.

When Sir Stafford Cripps became President of the Board of Trade in 1945, he had warned that clothes were going to remain in short supply, and on 11 August that year expressed doubt if the present ration could be maintained. At the time of Dior's first show in 1947 the Labour MP Mrs Mann asked him about improving the clothing ration. He wrote back on 14 February that clothes rationing must continue. An allowance of 32 coupons would start on 1 March and must last all year. That autumn he embarked on his austerity measures, and cut the clothing ration, the food ration, and the petrol

*13 **Dior strapless dinner dress, Richard Avedon, October 1947**, Harper's Bazaar. **The velvet bodice is heavily boned for support, and the skirt of faille silk is cut in deep petals, which are folded over each other, and cause movement when walking. The amount of silk required would have been considerable. As Dior concealed the legs more, he revealed the top for dinners.***

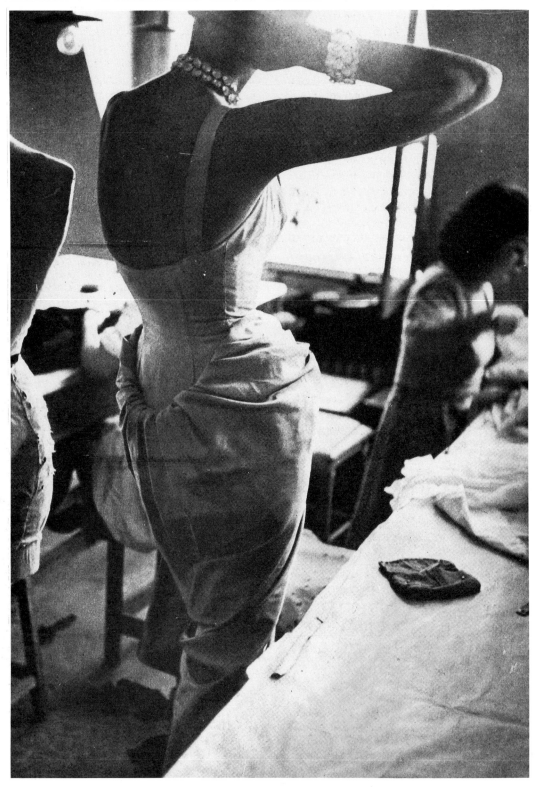

ration. In November 1947 Cripps was appointed Chancellor of the Exchequer, and declared 'While we are in this struggle none of us can afford to improve our standard of living, because we cannot make goods available for the home market, for some time to come.'[4]

Many Britons were unaware of Dior's existence. While the fashion magazines reported him, the newspapers did not, being full of dramas about the Deep Freeze in February 1947, with coal lorries and coal trains stuck in snow drifts, electricity cuts, and shops and offices trying to work by candlelight. The only gowns they featured were Molyneux's creations for the princesses, as the Royal Family embarked on Britain's last battleship HMS *Vanguard*, for a tour of South Africa.

Another person who tried to get the clothing ration increased was the fashion reporter Alison Settle, who went to tackle Sir Stafford Cripps in person.

'What New Look?' the minister demanded, not being a reader of fashion magazines. Miss Settle told him. 'Out of the question', the minister replied. Thoroughly displeased, Miss Settle told him that he was like King Canute trying to hold back the tides, for the New Look would flood in. Not while Cripps was at the Board of Trade.

The very first person Captain Molyneux's nephew Peter remembers wearing the New Look in London in 1947 was the public relations girl at Dereta. Everybody stared and asked what she was wearing.[5] How Dereta managed to find the fabric must remain a mystery, for all the company's records were destroyed when it was taken over by another firm in 1960. Elizabeth Ewing says Dereta produced 700 New Look suits in grey flannel which sold out in two weeks. It was a special line in unrationed fabric, outside the Utility Range, and could not be repeated, for unrationed clothes were strictly limited. If an ordinary dress using about 3 yards (2.7 metres) of material required 7 coupons, then a Dior day dress at 20 yards (18.3 metres) exceeded one persons's entire

14 *Inside Dior's workrooms, October 1947, Harper's Bazaar. Amidst all the full skirts there were a few narrow dresses, such as this evening gown. The bodice is boned, and the skirt is tight, and tucked into the descending waistline. The tables are covered with paper to keep the textiles clean, and to prevent them catching on splinters.*

15 *A cocktail dress, Seeberger Frères, September 1947. Not every model in the second collection dropped the hem to the ankle. This black cloth dress ends at the calf. It has a satin overblouse, trimmed with an enormous bow. This demonstrates Dior's tendency to spoil the line with a fussy feature, a characteristic which Molyneux disapproved of (Bibliothèque Nationale Paris).*

clothing coupon allowance. One would have to steal from other members of the family to obtain one. Judging from all the advertisements in the popular press for 1947, with the possible exception of Dereta, no British dress manufacturer attempted to produce the New Look. Ways would have to be found to achieve the style without using so much material.

The John Lewis Partnership presented a fashion show for the New Look in 1947 but for the staff in the Gown Department only. The report in the house *Gazette* states that it took place on 20 September, after Dior's second presentation. The text rightly points out that longer hemlines were being worn already for hems had dropped a year before.

John Lewis Fashion Parade.

Fashion has been international news lately, with Paris commanding the longer skirts, and America divided between those women who, anticipating Paris, have already been elegantly wearing the new length for months, and those who succeeded, from a variety of motives, in working themselves up to the point of hysterical demonstrations against it. In rugged England the situation may be visualized in Pantomime form, in which the Ugly Sisters, played to perfection by Sir Stafford and Dr Hugh, are seen sternly suppressing the feminine yearnings of poor little Cinderella. 'Long skirts indeed!' they cry with unusual co-ordination. 'Who are you to have fashionable skirts? Don't you known that your place is in the cinders? Any nice clothes that we may have are certainly not for you!'

The show was presented by a Miss Rowland who produced the new instrument of torture to achieve the Hour-Glass silhouette:

Miss Rowland, smiling more than ever, held up an enchanting little corset, pink satin and lace, which she assured us must be faced by all as the necessary foundation for the smart figure. This little garment was then girded on to a slim model with such vigour that the blood rushed to her face, while Miss Rowland exhorted her to greater efforts. 'Pull yourself in a little dear', and we all held our breaths in sympathy.

There was of course an enormous difference in putting corsets on a girl who had not worn them before, and the past approach when little girls were laced into corsets as soon as they could walk. Dior was trying to impose a handspan waist on a generation of women who had grown up without such constriction.

Before the parade proper began, Miss Rowland told us that its main object was to help us to have an intelligent knowledge of the new line and to be able to impart this knowledge to our customers. We should imagine today's line as a flower in which the pencil line represented the stem and the rounded hour-glass shape the petals.

At no time did the presenter use the term New Look, as that was not current until 1948. Unfortunately the report does not describe the dresses in detail except to say that some were cheap Utility models and others expensive rarities, and it does not mention when the clothes were to go on sale, but the end of 1947 looks likely. The models were two department managers, a buyer, two deputy buyers, a trainee, an assistant and three juniors.

1948 was definitely the year when the New Look was in all the shops. English *Vogue* Choice of the Month for June 1948 was a New Look handspan-waist suit-dress in white spotted navy rayon, which had a fitted jacket with basques and sloping shoulders, over a dress with a flared skirt to below the calf, over a taffeta petticoat, price £15 6s 7d available at Harvey Nichols, London, Bon Marché, Liverpool, and MacDonald's, Glasgow. This was an expensive version, but still slimmer than a voluminous Dior original.

New Looks in Utility versions were featured in a fashion show at Welwyn Stores, in Welwyn Garden City, in late September to October 1948. A full skirted afternoon dress in navy, yellow, and white Italian tie silk, still retained square shoulders with the longer hem. It was £5 17s 3d and seven coupons. A Harella Utility model coat, double-breasted, flared out in a wide, gored skirt below the calf, and was trimmed with a moleskin collar, but it too retained padded shoulders. It cost £6 19s 6d and 12 coupons. A conventional golfing suit in the same show only required four clothing coupons because it was constructed on the lean lines of the early 1940s with a narrow skirt and square shoulders, but it was expensive at £19 1s 5d for it employed brown Scottish tweed and a nappa jacket. Inevitably there was an overlap between the brand new examples with sloping shoulders available in metropolitan department stores of the higher grade, and the conservative square shouldered styles still on sale in the provinces. The New Look did not change the look of the population overnight. Longer hemlines were in fashion already, and it took a year for British industry to be able to put it on the market. Clothes rationing did not end until March 1949, and then it was voluminous skirts in all the stores. The impact of Dior can be seen in Carven, Dessès, Fath, Paquin and Piguet forming themselves into the Couturiers Associés in 1950, when John Lewis did business with them.[6]

The dress historian Avril Lansdell was a schoolgirl of 15 when the New Look came out in 1947, and she well remembers her mother's look of stunned disbelief when they first saw the Dior photographs in the magazines. 'Where are we going to get the fabric to make that?' her mother exclaimed, for she made her own and her daughter's clothes. Many British women said they would refuse to wear the New Look because of the difficulties it involved. Their teenage daughters felt differently. They were just at the age when they wanted to identify their own generation, so the New Look was their uniform, no matter how problematic it might prove to achieve. Fortunately as it was now peacetime the blackout curtains could come down. Avril Lansdell's very first New Look skirt was made by her mother from blackout material, trimmed with coloured bands of bias binding round the bottom. She wore it to a peasant dance at a Girl Guides' concert, and afterwards wore it with a white blouse. George VI expected his daughters Princess Elizabeth and Princess Margaret Rose to obey the clothing restrictions, and their couturier Captain Molyneux showed how by taking an existing coat of Princess Margaret's, and inserting some velvet bands to widen the skirt and lower the hem. This example showed many women how to tackle the problems. In spring 1948 some longer dresses did appear in the shops, and Butterick Paper Patterns published a method of making a New Look dress from two old ones, so Avril's mother bought it. She took one of Avril's school frocks in brown check gingham, and one of her own brown linen dresses, and created a dress with a brown linen bodice and bottom half of the skirt, and a check top half of the skirt matched with cap sleeves in the check. Avril wore it to school and was summoned before the headmistress to explain her appearance. Avril said sweetly 'I've grown three inches since last summer, and this was the best my Mother could do as she has no coupons to spare.' This argument worked, so other sixth formers started copying Avril's dress. Some strange concoctions were the result but the older girls succeeded in wearing longer hems to school. For sport the school's gym slips were actually four inches above the knee.

The summer of 1948 saw the coronation

of Queen Juliana of the Netherlands, and Avril Lansdell went over because her brother's Boy Scout troupe was twinned with a Dutch troupe. For the trip her mother bought her first dress from a shop, a £6 Horrock's cotton New Look, plus coupons. She found that Dutch girls had managed to achieve the New Look by using patchwork. They took six inch (15 cm) squares of any fabrics and sewed them all up, to make a long skirt, but the edging had to be in the national colour orange. Sewing thread was unobtainable so they were unpicking old clothes for the thread. Dutch girls topped their patchwork skirts with ex US Army T-shirts, a foretaste of teenage styles in the Fifties. Ingenuity was the key for most women wanting the New Look under rationing, as when Avril's mother took her short dirndl skirt with horizontal stripes, unpicked it, and turned the fabric round to create a narrow, long skirt of vertical stripes. Avril at 16 felt very grown up in that. In 1949 she began her arts course at Ealing Art School.[7]

In France the German rationing system collapsed in 1944 with the Liberation, but great shortages dominated the following years. France was a wreck, looted by the Nazis, her industry rundown, and the Allies and the French Resistance had bombed ports, bridges and railways. No trains ran from Paris to Lyon and Marseilles in 1944/5. De Gaulle re-established a government, and in 1947 Jean Monnet came up with a reconstruction plan, with housing as the first priority. 1947 was also the year of the severe winter which ruined spring crops, and Europe lacked the money to pay for imported food, so the situation was grave. The USA began to realise that Europe would have to be rebuilt if she was to resist Communism, so the Marshall Plan was established in March 1948. France received 140,000,000 old francs in 1948, and 263,000,000 old francs in 1949. Consequently Dior launched his New Look into a country which was existing on American charity.[8]

The New Look was not the instant success which subsequent historians have termed it, for the simple reason that there was not the fabric in 1947 for its general adoption. It was not until 1948 that the style became more obvious in England, Holland, Germany and France, but there were still shortages.

Matters were much easier in the USA. Rationing had been less total, and factories had not been blitzed. They were also better informed, for the *New York Herald Tribune* (now the *International Herald Tribune*) had a European edition, which gave, and still gives, thorough reports on every Paris collection, as well as publishing all the times and dates of the shows, with the supplementary shows by the glovers, shoemakers, milliners and textile houses all with their new lines. It admitted that America had become very fashion orientated on New York during the war, and not many buyers had woken up to the fact that Paris was open for all the world, and not simply its Nazi customers. On 6 August Lucie Noel reported that a huge number of American buyers were on their way on the SS *America* for the autumn collections 1947, with Dior particularly in mind. She described his second collection as 'breath-taking and supremely elegant', and said of the wide skirts, 'fullness is circular, sunray-pleated, box pleated, or obtained by massed godet, back or front.' She even listed all the buyers in town, from as far away as California.[9] In 1947 that meant a train journey across the USA and then a liner across the Atlantic. Who had persuaded buyers to undertake such an epic trip? Dior's public relations officer, Harrison Elliot, who was an American. The targeting of Dior on the USA was his work, and he had circularized every buyer in the States who worked for an important store. The granting of Dior scents English names, and the opening of the first Dior branches in New York, would all show the imprint of Harrison Elliot, a factor absent from the Dior exhibition in Paris in 1987.

Harrison Elliot had been sent to France as a GI with the US Army. After the war, like a number of young men from as far away as Australia or the USA, he decided to remain in Europe for a period, and find a job. Maison Dior, brand new, needed an English speaking representative to deal with the American market. Harrison Elliot was their man.

In September 1947 Dior sailed to the United States on the *Queen Elizabeth* for Nieman Marcus of Dallas had awarded him its 'Oscar for Couture'. Dior said in his autobiography, that he chose a British ship because he loved things English, England's tradition, English politeness, English architecture, and strangely enough for a Frenchman, English food. He doted on Yorkshire pudding, mincepies, roast chicken with stuffing, and delighted in the English breakfast with tea, porridge, eggs and bacon. This shows Dior's Norman background, for the Normans are conscious of their ties across the Channel, and do not treat the subject of England with the dismissive shrug of a Frenchman born far inland.[10]

Dior found the United States intimidating

16 Stanley Marcus confers the first 'Oscars for Fashion', September 1947. This was Dior's first visit to the USA and the Nieman Marcus store, Dallas, awarded him its Oscar 'for continuing the great traditions of French fashion'. Norman Hartnell was honoured 'for his undoubted supremacy in English feminine fashion' as dressmaker to Queen Elizabeth. The photograph shows, from left to right; Major Mitchenson, representing Norman Hartnell; Salvatore Ferragamo, who got an award for 'his inventive genius and original creation in the field of feminine footwear'; Stanley Marcus; Irene, honoured for 'her creative fantasy in her models for Hollywood stars'; and lastly Dior (Photograph courtesy of Salvatore Ferragamo SpA, Florence).

"NEIMAN MARCUS„ - STATI UNITI AMERICA

FONDAZIONE PER IL RICONOSCIMENTO E PREMIAZIONE DEI MIGLIORI ARTISTI NEL CAMPO INTERNAZIONALE DELLA MODA

17 *Dior cocktail gown with Ferragamo shoes.*
Another Dior garment in the Oscar show,
September 1947. This model in black cloth has a
crystal bedecked neckline, and a sloping
hemline – shades of the 1927–9 dip. The dress is
lined with silk, and has a dipping petticoat
(Photograph courtesy of Salvatore Ferragamo
SpA, Florence).

and overwhelming. A shy person, he was
alarmed by reporters at the quayside
demanding how dare he drop hemlines
and conceal women's legs? On being
informed of the 300,000 girls who were
joining 'Little Below the Knee' clubs, he
replied that those who protested loudest
would end-up wearing the longest skirts.
In Chicago he was greeted with women
carrying placards saying 'Down with the
New Look', 'Burn Monsieur Dior', 'Christian
Dior Go Home'. The presentation in Dallas
in Texas was a gala event draped in cloth

of gold, but Dior was very glad to return to
quieter Europe. The American press noted
that he was 5 feet 5 inches tall, with blue
eyes, and light brown hair, and weighed
145 pounds. His hair had begun to recede
from the forehead in his twenties, and
once he gained a regular job at Piguet's,
Dior had acquired the pear-shaped
silhouette he retained for the remainder of
his life, for he liked food.

Back in Paris the company had not been
idle. Jacques Rouët had organized two new
departments, Christian Dior Furs, and in
October 1948 Christian Dior Perfumes was
established as a company under the
management of Heftler Louiche, and
launched Miss Dior as its first scent. The
English name was significant with the
wealthy American market clearly in mind.
The stables at the back of the mansion in
the avenue Montaigne were demolished,
and work started on the construction of a
seven-storey extension for Maison Dior.
Marcel Boussac increased his investment
from 10 million francs in 1947, to 100
million francs in 1949 for he had found
himself a winner. Thus unlike other
couture houses Dior was introducing
subsidiary departments in its first year.

For spring 1948 Dior showed his Zig Zag
Line and his Flight Line. The first, he
wrote: 'gives to robes, wide or narrow, the
movement and nervous character of a
sketch'. And of Flight: 'an unequally spread
amplitude, which flies out when the
wearer is walking and plunges towards the
rear'. The Zig Zag was best seen in a plain
skirt with over-panels with sloping hems.
These panels were turned back upon
themselves, and so created the descending
Z in their hems, on top of the plain skirt
beneath. The idea probably came from the
way a shawl folds back upon itself, for
shawls were a fashionable accessory back
in his childhood. Flight was expressed in
fly-out jackets, stiffed with buckram, worn
over narrow skirts, and producing backs
which stood out from the waist, like a flare

of fabric. An example was *Aventure*, a narrow black dress in woollen cloth, with a jacket with a flared back of godets in chicken's-foot yellow. Hemlines in general varied from model to model. Evening dresses showed the ankle, and Dior's beloved bustle effects continued in the back spread of pleats. The evening dress *Martinique* was a strapless corsage over an ankle-length skirt in striped organza. A panel in front was pleated from the waist, and at the back a longer panel with more pleats cascaded to the ground recalling Worth's fan shaped hems of 1873. Dior said that a geometric rigour dominated the cut of the collection, but there was some drapery left in the afternoon dress *Drag* in marine-blue mohair with long sleeves, and a full skirt draped at the hips, as if pulled up and held, like irregular folds.

In May 1948 the New Look received royal approbation for Princess Elizabeth wore it on her official visit to Paris, but in a British version. David Perlman reported in the *New York Herald Tribune* that she presented 'the London Look'. Her aides explained that this was a conservative version of the New Look, with the hemline just below the calves and not around the ankles as Dior had just introduced. Princess Elizabeth wore the London look in the morning in a dove-grey coat, with a tight waist, and calf-length hem, with which she wore a hat with a veil, decked with roses. After lunch she changed to open the exhibition on British life, and wore a slate blue ottoman silk dress with drapery around the hips, and a slightly flared skirt terminating below the calf.

18 **A Dior cocktail gown with Ferragamo sandals. At the Oscars there was a fashion parade of the prizewinners' models. Sensibly Dior has allowed the fabric to dominate, so that the paisley pattern is revealed. Dior could achieve the discipline characteristic of Molyneux sometimes (Photograph courtesy of Salvatore Ferragamo SpA, Florence).**

Model Abandon, *autumn–winter 1948. While it appeared in his Winged Line,* Abandon *was an early hint of the Oblique and Illusion Lines to come, with its neckline cut off one shoulder. Black cloth was a favourite fabric for Dior. He raised hemlines to 14 in (35 cm) from the ground (Musée des Arts de la Mode, Paris).*

19 **Princess Elizabeth with Pierre de Gaulle, Lord Mayor of Paris, 14 May 1948. British designers refused to drop hems to the ankle, and Princess Elizabeth took the London length to Paris on her first official visit, when she opened an exhibition at the Musée Galliera on Eight Centuries of British Life. Her hemline was just below the calf. Dior took note (Associated Press photograph).**

With it went a cartwheel hat in straw trimmed with tulle and lilies-of-the-valley. Her wardrobe was by Molyneux.[11]

The London look was hemlines at 12 to 14 inches (30–36 cm) from the ground. England's couturiers did not imitate Dior's ankle length hems, but evolved a sensible compromise between the short skirts of 1946 and Dior's ankle skimmers of autumn 1947, which Princess Elizabeth displayed to the French. Her example, and the huge storm of criticism from Britain and the USA made an impact. For his autumn collections 1948, Dior raised his hem to 14 inches (36 cm) from the ground. He launched his Winged Line, a follow-on from his Flight Line, and the Cyclonic Line, and wrote in his programme that hems were no longer important,

> *This season, the interest is no longer in the length of skirts, but in the cut and the distribution of the excitedly drawn amplitude, and no longer wavey or loose. This measured fullness allows movement with ease, and without embarrassment.*
>
> *The waist is well marked and retains its natural suppleness.*
>
> *The line fleeing from the shoulders is accentuated by a new cut of the sleeve. This cut frequently causes the effect of wings, of an uplifting which gives the bust an interest not expressed in past seasons.*
>
> *We have attempted to give the silhouette the maximum amount of youth and unconstraint.*

Of the accompanying Cyclonic Line Dior only said that it employed a technique to

increase the size of dance skirts, but he did not explain what this technique was. He was already using horsehair petticoats to extend skirts but whether he was now introducing ribs of sprung steel from the crinoline, he did not say. The colours for winter were coal black, anthracite black, warm brown, grey, and a cindered beige, lighted by a bluish flame, the pinks and reds. The jewellery colours were inspired by Byzantine art.

The dress *Girouette*, Weathercock, best illustrated the cyclonic element Dior intended. It had a strapless bodice of black velvet, and a skirt of black taffeta heavily reinforced with thick horsehair into huge folds, which overlapped each other, to create a permanent shape. Dior was attempting to freeze the wild impact of a cyclone on to a dress.

The winged effect was not only expressed in sleeves, but in skirts. The model *Cocotte* had a winged bustle, formed by a plain skirt with pleats in the back, overlaid with two layers of aprons, as in the 1870s; these were long enough to be pulled round to the rear as two standing wings over the backside. Buckram lining would have been necessary, and it shows Dior always willing to recycle nineteenth-century styles, in a new way. *Harper's Bazaar* noted Dior's introduction of strapless dresses for restaurants, citing his petal folds which encircled skirts with deep, swinging layers. It cheered the fact that Paris was copying London's hemlines, and thought the most important trend was the small hats in the collection. This was a significant change. Hats in the 1940s had been the turban for everyday, and the cartwheel for events, but now a very small hat was being promoted by Mitzah Bricard at Dior's. This required small, neat hairstyles so the long locks of the 1940s were on the way out. Next year the ballerina Zizi Jeanmaire began to sport the *gamine* look, with the hair cropped to about three inches long, so the new style

was given a lot of publicity.

That October saw Dior opening in the USA with Christian Dior Perfumes New York Inc. at 730 Fifth Avenue, and on 28 October the opening of Christian Dior New York Inc. at Fifth Avenue and 57 Street, to sell luxury ready-to-wear and accessories. Dior had been impressed by the wealth of the USA on his tour the year before, and had advised Rouët to start foreign branches there. The house was being so successful that Dior bought himself a country retreat, the old mill at Coudret, Milly la Forêt, near Fontainebleau, where he created a very English lawn, and flowerbeds, notably absent in usual French gardens. Dior was again expressing his liking for English ways. He liked to say that he had two green thumbs, and henceforth would escape the pressures of Paris by gardening, experimenting with vegetables and flowers, and trying to improve fruit trees. His spell as market gardener had taken deep roots.

On 8 February 1949 Dior showed his spring and summer collections with his Trompe L'Oeil or Illusion Line, and his Foreign Line. He wrote that

This new collection is based on two principles of illusion; the one, by various effects of pockets and looseness gives the bust a bloom and breadth which however respects the natural curve of the shoulders; the other, allowing the body its line, leads on skirts to fullness and indispensable movement. The line illusion has as its aim the necessary corrections of the silhouette to give fabric all its value, while leaving the body its suppleness and to movement all its liberty.

He said that hemlines, now sensibly shortened, were no longer an issue. Illusion he expressed in false pockets on the breast of a jacket, or in button pockets placed on the hips, where they evoked the allure of the gauchos (of Argentina). Illusion lay in the layers of petals he placed on evening skirts, which with movement and dancing, would flutter. Illusion removed tailored collars from suits. The Foreign Line was however shown by very large revers on jackets and coats, where the style was intended to convey the hastily thrown on foreign jacket. He did not specify which nation's jackets he was thinking of, but possibly something of a Magyar dolman may have been in mind. Evidently he had spent the winter studying foreign dress for inspiration.

Colours for spring were based completely on flowers and vegetation. There was the white of lilies of the valley, raw white and white hyacinth, the pink and reds of peonies and roses, the violet of violets and lilac and clematis, the yellow of primulas, the blue of cornflowers and forget-me-nots, the red of poppies and geraniums, the green of grass, the straw yellow of ripe wheat, but tailored suits were still in blacks, greys, marine blue and beige.

Harper's Bazaar noted the use of flying panels to soften his tubular skirts in what it dubbed his 'vol-au-vent' look, and Dior used panels again in his autumn collection 1949. For the Centre of the Century Dior displayed his Scissor Line and Windmill-in-the-Wind Line, where stiffened panels crossed over each other like scissor blades, or windmill blades echoed in panels spread across a skirt in a semi-circle. It was underlined by the use of contrasting fabrics, so that a dress in cloth had satin scissor panels, velvet was set against wool, satin against velvet. These, Dior said were the principal themes of the collection. The dominant winter shade was black with strong grey, and uranium grey. Evening wear had a Dior red that he claimed as his own, tender pink, gold, blueish green and enamel blue, chestnut, marine blue, and touches of orange and green. The press observed the huge shawl collars appearing on coats, which were mostly loose and voluminous. Several coats Dior said were indebted to shepherds' houppelandes, the

21 **Dior evening gown, Seeberger Frères, September 1948. This satin gown has a stole draped over the shoulders and round the waist, terminating in one of Dior's favourite bows. Twisted round the torso it was representative of Dior's Cyclonic Line (Bibliothèque Nationale Paris).**

rough cloaks worn by shepherds in bad weather. He tried to convey the primitive nature of these loose garments in his full coats.

Several Illusion gowns survived into the autumn collection. *Peruvian* was a black satin entirely covered with black satin leaves, with clusters at the upper arm. It was an ankle length evening gown. Larger petal shapes were featured on *Venus*, in pink tulle with embroidered leaves or petals cascading down into a train. *Juno* in blue grey tulle also had large petals encrusted with embroidered sequins round the hems. In contrast to dresses with windmill panels and scissor shapes, or petals and leaves, there was one shirtwaister in the collection with a pleated skirt and long sleeves, which was a pointer to the more simple shapes that Dior would turn to in the Fifties.[12]

1949 also saw the first stocking licence in the USA with Julius Kayser & Co. to make Christian Dior Hosiery. Dior Perfumes brought out its second scent Diorama. Parisian high society was anxious to regain its reputation as the capital of pleasure, so in 1949 Comte Etienne de Beaumont staged a fancy dress ball, the ball of kings and queens, and he invited Dior, for Dior was reviving luxury dress. The couturier went as the king of beasts, with a lion's head in papier maché, a long cloak, evening dress adorned with epaulettes, and fake orders of chivalry. It was designed by Pierre Cardin who had spent two years as a leading hand in the tailoring workroom at Maison Dior, but who had just left to set up business as a theatrical costumier in the rue Richepanse, so Dior gave him this helping hand by wearing his creation. Following this successful event there was to be a rash of lavish balls and fancy dress parties given by the rich during the 1950s, with Dior of course designing many of the gowns.

Dior had set out to restructure women and had largely succeeded by 1950 when the New Look was adopted widely in the West, albeit with British hems at 12 to 14 inches (30-36 cm) from the ground. Many women attempted to reduce their waistlines, and returned to corsets, hip frills, and horsehair petticoats to achieve the new silhouette, especially in the United States where there was no rationing. For women with angular shoulders there was no way that they could fit into Dior's sloping shoulderlines, except by raising the neckline to start the slope higher up. There are always some people who suit one fashion, but not the next one, because their basic bone structure cannot be modified (except by drastic surgery). Dior who considered that he had the right to reconstruct women, to accord with his ideals about them, made no attempt to restructure himself, and his own waistline expanded in the opposite direction to that which he asked of women. For the petite figure Dior was found ideal. The ballerina Margot Fonteyn bought the suit *Daisy* at the first collection in 1947, and became a regular customer thereafter. Several of her Dior gowns are at the Museum of Costume, Bath (see Appendix II). Captain Molyneux retired in 1950, so one finds his royal client Princess Margaret transferring to Dior for her 21st birthday ballgown in 1951. The Duchess of Windsor had expressed doubts about the New Look when it was first launched, but she became a customer once the fuss had died down.

This frustrated architect had rebuilt women as corollas, lianas, flowers, figures of eight, the back of Paris, zigzags, cyclones, as wings, as flight, as illusions, scissors, windmills, foreigners, so what would he do with them in the Fifties?

3

Dior in the Fifties

Dior declared in his spring collection 1950, 'The collection is above all *1950*. It is constructed on the theme of the Vertical Line. This line, clear and stripped of inessentials, confirms the tendency hinted at for two seasons, and remains essentially feminine, for it is intended to make women value Woman.'

On dresses, bodices were moulded like sweaters, and were often sleeveless, and the necklines plunged down like bathing costumes. Dior dubbed this the Horseshoe Neckline, and said it was to emphasize the bust. The overall figure was narrow, and this was seen above all in the skirts, and although some had pleats and godets, these were not allowed to go beyond the line of the hips. Bodices and skirts were both often worked over with pleats or ribbing, to demonstrate the 'fairy fingers': the traditional name for Parisian couture. Raglan sleeves were employed. The coats were longer than in the last collections, with low set pockets, and some were three-quarters or half length. The dustcoats in shantung were widely reported by the press. Some coats were made from three or four panels set at right angles to the lie of the fabric, which produced a voluminous result.

On suits, the Horseshoe Neckline was expressed in bolero or spencer jackets, with short sleeves. The skirts were narrow. The aim was to convey the negligent elegance of sailorboys and sailorgirls, doubtless remembered from Normandy. For early evening, dinner and cabaret visits, Dior offered short gowns in muslin and taffeta, with the hem near the calf. For the grand evening dress embroidery, brocades and fullness provided the fairy-like transformation, but the line still followed the simple outlines of day dress. In fabrics, Dior made a radical change to muslins, georgettes, organza and taffetas, all in silk. Great use of ribbons created a raying effect on pleated muslins. Patterns, Dior stated, were chiefly based on the harlequinade, or on bestiaries. Navy blue contrasted with white dominated the daywear, with black and white coming second. The white ranged over to grey, ivory and beige. Hats were small or straw boaters, another nautical touch, and he included a collapsible umbrella hat which could be fitted into a pocket when dry.

The look for autumn–winter 1950 Dior

22 **Dior's Oblique Line, Seeberger Frères, February 1950.** The printed corsage ends in a twisted knot on the right hip, but at the back continues down to ground level. It is the eighteenth-century fashion for showing the petticoat, interpreted in an evening gown, where the petticoat of net is exposed in front and on the right side, and concealed on the left side and back. This dress from the spring collection was a prototype, for the Oblique Line was not announced until the autumn collection (Bibliothèque Nationale Paris).

named Oblique, expressed in pediments and raised collars, and the Enfolded or Interlaced Line. By the architectural pediment, Dior meant the woman's face at the top, the shoulders representing the base, and he said it was 'audacity joined to dignity'. It is an early hint of his A Line, narrow at the top and wide at the bottom, but Dior did not identify the dress with this look. Oblique fastening of the collars was a strong feature, and scarf collars draped across the torso expressed the line too, as on the suit *Favori* in grey flannel,

and the black coat *New York*. The pediment was seen on the suit *London* in black cloth, which had a triangular fastening over the chest, outlined with buttons. It had short sleeves, and a narrow skirt, with two long pockets at each hip also outlined by buttons. Shawl collars on coats, and buttons were obliquely set, or else in a pediment arrangement. Three-quarter-length coats were intended for day dresses, and contrasted their volume with the slenderness beneath. Dior said some sleeves were cut as elephant ears, so they were presumably quite large.

In evening gowns full skirts outnumbered narrow. Some had oblique scarves crossing on the bodice and widening out to form full skirts or large basques. These expressed the Interlaced Line. There was also the Lily-of-the-Valley Line in 1950, shown on day dresses which widened at the base, and spread out like fans. The colours were glorious black, Dior's favourite, royal white, Dior red, and violet vervain.

The theme for spring 1951 was the Oval Line, constructed on the Natural Line, declared Dior. The oval of the face, of the bust and of the hips is superimposed on the collection to follow the natural curves of the feminine body. Shoulders were suppressed by deeply excavated sleeveheads, and Dior named the cut chicken's thigh, for it was wide at the top and narrowed near the elbow. The curve now dominated the collection. *Harper's Bazaar* in April 1951 noted that the look was now less sculpted, with lower shoulders, and softer basques on jackets. The dustcoats, in silk or shantung, continued voluminous, and were intended to be worn over summer dinner dresses, such as a strapless dress in piqué embroidered with dragonflies. *Elle* illustrated an example *Biarritz* in blue shantung. The Oblique still lingered on in evening wear, with the strapless gown in silver embroidered organza, *Puccini*, having

a waist sash which expanded and fell on
the right hip into floating panels to the
hem. A strapless gown in black taffeta,
tightly moulded to the bust and hips, had
an obliquely set, interlaced overskirt of
tulle, which flared out on each hip in
unequal lengths. The Horseshoe Neckline
was still in existence, on the dress in iron
grey alpaca with a spencer jacket in beige
shantung. This was worn with a wide,
featured, with the *Fine Party* short evening
dress having an obliquely crossed over
shawl collar, terminating at the waistline,
where a pleated skirt flared, all in ivory silk
shantung, which was worn with a wide,
cocktail hat in black net. Dior reserved
pleating for the light fabrics, preferably
patterned. Lengths varied from model to
model. Some day dresses had hems at the

24 *Dior summer dress, Seeberger Frères, February
1950. Enormous pockets were a feature of the
spring–summer collection in 1950. Here they
reach down to the hem. They also appeared on
some suits, where the jacket was elongated into a
tunic with enormous pockets down to the hem,
partially concealing the skirt. The neckline shows
the Horseshoe Neck which featured in this
collection (Bibliothèque Nationale Paris).*

23 *Dior day dress, Seeberger Frères, February
1950. This outfit has all the simplicity Molyneux
preached, and shows Dior could reach his idol's
standards when he tried. The dress is plain, with
only the collar and cuffs as features. Hemlines
were raised to just below the knee, after the
outcry over Dior's ankle-length hemlines
(Bibliothèque Nationale Paris).*

calf, others nearer the knee, so Dior was
undecided where to set them, in view of
all the fuss over his hems in 1947. For
colour he chose the light grey of Ile de
France, presumably meaning the sky, and
fresh black. From this spring–summer
collection Princess Margaret ordered her
21st birthday ballgown, which was of
white silk organza, embroidered with
flowers and foliage in straw tone, spangles,
and mother-of-pearl. The bodice had an
Oblique arrangement with one shoulder
strap on the left shoulder, embroidered
like an epaulette, and the line crossing the

chest at a descending angle. It is now in the Museum of London.

For the autumn 1951 Dior announced his Long Line, 'from the hat to the shoes, it is an entirely new proportion which ends the evolution inherited from preceding collections.' Length was achieved by removing the basques from suit jackets, to make the skirt seem longer. Jackets and sleeves were generally cut on the bias to round the bust gently. There were lots of short spencer jackets still retained, which also produced a long silhouette in the skirt. This long look was inspired by the Directoire and Empire periods in France, when the classical high waist had been the fashion. Dior did not go all out for a higher waistline, but there were hints of it. Loose jackets had a strap across the back at Empire level. Some evening gowns had both the fitted waist for which Dior was known, and the Empire line marked by a contrasting band of colour. The main cut for dresses was the princess line, Worth's invention to avoid waistlines, but the dresses still flared out in the familiar Dior style. The Empire hint was a bow at bust level. Coats were mostly the redingote or overcoat of classic British invention, but very full, with the buttons in diverging lines, widening out down the coat. This provided the wide base for the Long Line, and is an indication of the A line concept

26 *Dior's Long Line, Seeberger Frères, autumn 1951. The long silhouette was achieved by narrowing the line, so this suit has a slender skirt topped by a hip-length jacket. The petal type pockets are an echo of the larger ones of 1950. There is a hint of widening the shoulders which was taken further in Dior's Tulip and Magnet lines. Slenderness was replacing the full skirt of 1947 (Bibliothèque Nationale Paris).*

25 *HRH Princess Margaret Rose in her Dior birthday gown, Cecil Beaton, 1951. As the designer to the princesses, Captain Molyneux retired in 1950, Princess Margaret transferred to Dior, significantly for her 21st birthday ballgown. The single epaulette and the front panel are embroidered with straw, spangles, mother-of-pearl, in a floral pattern. The bodice has eight whalebones, and the neckline is in the Oblique style, descending from the epaulette and sleeve set at the left shoulder, across to the right cap sleeve which is down at the elbow. The bodice and central panel are in organza, but the skirt and four petticoats are in nylon (Camera Press Ltd).*

to come. Evening gowns mostly had bolero jackets or scarves, and for grand occasions were all long. Black was the chief tone, black velvet, black cloth, black taffeta, black satin, black silk. It was contrasted with green in all its range from emerald to dull bronze, and Spanish moss. Dior red and spice yellow were employed as decorations. The Empire look was often no more than a chestnut velvet bow on the bust of a normal waisted, full skirted evening gown like *Mexico*, embroidered in gold thread. *Venezuela* was a full skirted gown of red organza, with a sash and bow

27 **Dior suit, Seeberger Frères, winter 1951. This example of the Long Line retains an Oblique feature in the curved revers, which seem to reach for the left of the waist, but is cut back to button at centre front. The four buttoned pockets show Dior still playing with that feature. The skirt is narrow (Bibliothèque Nationale Paris).**

28 **Dior evening gown, Seeberger Frères, winter 1950–1. The Long Line for evening, showing the Empire waistline where the embroidery is heaviest, and still curved into the natural waist. The gown is black velvet embroidered by d'Eichthal in silver droplets, and has a stole of velvet edged with fur. Dior was cautiously edging towards changes at the waist (Bibliothèque Nationale Paris).**

of red faille set at Empire level, with the ends falling down to the floor. Dior appears to have listened to Captain Molyneux's advice: do not introduce new looks overnight and upset the whole industry, think ahead, and plan a new line by gradual hints over the seasons. This sort of disciplined approach was not instinctive to Dior, but he did consult Molyneux, from time to time and these Empire signs were a first indication of a general narrowing of the mode to come, introduced by gentle hints, in the Molyneux manner.

In spring 1952 Dior displayed his Sinuous Line, with its chief effect of youthful informality with sweaters and *blousons*, loose jackets which were fitted at the waist. Dresses now lost collars for a simple stripe copied from cardigans. Cloth shaped sweaters topped suits, with V necks and short sleeves. Shoulders were natural with no shaping. Many dresses had imitation blouson tops, which could be removed to convert them into cocktail dresses. These sweaters and blousons completely replaced spencers and bolero jackets. Some sweaters reached down to the hips, as did some blousons, so for the first time since 1947, Dior was ignoring the tight, normal waistline in both his collections for 1952. Waists at the Empire level and waists at the hips, show the corseted waist being avoided. Dior was turning away from his flower woman to a stalk woman. This was the biggest change in his development as a designer.

The dominant tones were neutral, grey, caramel, chestnut, beige, plus the standard black, in the daywear mostly. Dior red, azalea, mauve, begonia pink, hydrangea blue, daffodil yellow and grass green were for the end of summer evenings. Once again horticulture makes an impact. Dior did dub the whole collection the Sinuous Line, but its expression in sweaters and blousons may mean a general ease of fit, rather than any waving styles, which he did not show.

For the autumn of 1952 Dior looked to the Profiled Line and the Loose or Soft Cut as his principal themes. Length was still important and hems were 4 inches (10 cm) longer than in the previous collection. Jackets dispensed with buttons to produce an unbroken silhouette. Dresses had sashes and half belts set high, still with the Empire influence, to create length. Dior wrote, 'wide or narrow, they profiled themselves with the living precision of aeroplanes or motorcars.' So he was trying to achieve a streamlined effect. He launched his chemise dress, which had two shoulder straps, and a bodice and skirt of pleated grey silk. Over it went a short, fitted jacket. He showed a multi-layer combination of a stole-cum-jacket with enormous pockets, which fitted over another jacket on a chemise dress. Spencers were revived for evening gowns, and the overall style was slimming down. Evening gowns were less full, and were frequently accompanied by long stoles. The dress *Indecision* in grey crepe consisted entirely of pleating, set both straight and obliquely on the bodice, and straight on the skirt which reached down below the calf. In violent contrast to the general look, Dior also showed some paniered skirts for evening, with widely stiffened sides. Some had shortish hems and rather lacked elegance. *Elle* featured Dior's leopard prints that autumn, and they also appeared in the film *Gentlemen Marry Brunettes* (the other half of Anita Loos' statement that they prefer blondes) where Dior dressed Jane Russell and Jeane Crain in tight, 1930s type, evening gowns in leopard print. The news from corset makers was of the new long girdle which was essential to Dior's slimmer silhouettes.

The stalk woman reached her culmination in spring 1953 with the Tulip Line. Dior wrote: 'The new line consecrates the complete overthrowal of proportion, the expansion of the bust, and the effacement of the hips.' He declared

1   Evening dress 'Ispahan' worn in the 'Revue Adam', autumn-winter
1947. Illustration by René Gruau.

2 and 3   A fashion feature in *Plaisir de France*, December 1947, headed
'…. in their fantasy disguises'. These two Dior designs were called
'The Cossack' and 'Whirling Dervish'.

fantasques "

4. la gitane

3. le derviche tourneur

1. CHRISTIAN DIOR
2. PIERRE BALMAIN
3. CHRISTIAN DIOR
4. MAGGY ROUFF

Composition de Baumgartner.

CHRISTIAN DIOR

4   The French caption to this illustration by Reinolo from *Femina*,
October 1947, reads: 'The fullness of the back is prominent in certain
evening dresses. In this one the lightly swathed hips are adorned with a
drape of pale pink satin.

5   Ball Gown in blue-violet organdie. Dior stated that hemlines,
now sensibly shortened, were no longer an issue. Illustration from
Femina, June 1949.

6   Dior evening dress in black satin with pleated drapery bustle effect,
c. 1949.

7   'Le chapeau bleu'. Illustration by René Gruau from *Femina*,
April 1949.

Eau de toilette "*Miss Dior*"
Parfums Christian Dior

8   Advertisement for 'Miss Dior' by René Gruau in the June 1949 edition
of *Femina*. Miss Dior was the first scent of Christian Dior Perfumes which
had been set up in October 1948 under the guidance of Jacques Rouet.

that his new wide tops would make breathing easier, but omitted that his very tight skirts would impede movement. This could be seen in a black and white tweed suit which had a very loose jacket to the hips, but a very tight skirt below. It was shown on a black wool suit, with a wasp waisted jacket to the hips, bulbous short sleeves, and an arrow slim skirt. Dresses were made to similar narrow extremes, with only the top loose. Some evening gowns were equally slender, one being in black faille, with a white organdie bow at the bust, which was easier in fit. Some full skirts remained for evening, but were out-numbered by the narrower ones. Neutral tones were dispensed with this season, and black and grey led, with spring green as the chief contrast. For summery evenings Dior again looked to the corolla, as well as tulips and the iris for yellow, vermilion, pink and pale blue.

The slender line affected coats as well, so that the evening coat in black taffeta was gathered in at the neck, and fell into a modest spread. The coat *Rose Pompon* was completely straight to the calf, with a sloping shoulder line indicative of the tulip, and low set sleeves. There were still some oblique touches. *May*, a strapless evening gown in ivory organza embroidered in green silks with grapes, leaves and flowers, had the bodice fastened obliquely across the front to fix at the right waist. Another evening gown, *Mexico*, echoed Worth's tunic dresses, by having a skirt and overskirt, in white silk muslin, printed with festoons in grey, where the overskirt had a very oblique hem

encircling the underskirt. Lines don't disappear just because the fashion press says so.

The narrow and the full both appeared in the autumn collection for 1953. Dior's Living Line was inspired by the Eiffel Tower and the domes of Paris, so the frustrated architect again looked to architecture and engineering. The hemline of this look was the shortest in Paris, to just below the knee. Dior's greatest rival in the Fifties, Balenciaga of the sculptural suits, dropped his hemlines to the bottom

*30 **Dior's Tulip Line, Seeberger Frères, July 1953. Bulk and width are now placed across the shoulders and bust, while the waist, hips and legs are streamlined into a stalk. The jacket shows Dior's use of blouson jackets with buttoned cuffs and high-fastened neck, and the looseness which he retains at the top, but below the bust he narrows the blouson dramatically, to terminate at the hips. This look would occur again in his Magnet Line (Bibliothèque Nationale Paris).***

*29 **Dior's Sinuous Line, Seeberger Frères, August 1952. By sinuous Dior meant easier to wear, and the line was more relaxed than was usual in his collections, but here it is expressed in a wavy pattern on an evening gown, which is appliquéd with silver bands edged with silver fringe. The volume of his skirts is beginning to reduce (Bibliothèque Nationale Paris).***

of the calf, but Dior's short hems would become the principal level for the remainder of the Fifties among the young. The Eiffel Tower, a forecast of the A line to come, was expressed in dresses and suits which were still strongly tulip in outline, very slim over the hips and easier at the top. Jackets regained basques, but many were cut loose in the blouson style, and many had no collars, still reflecting the loss of that item from the sweaters and blousons of 1952. Decorative bands appeared across the collection. The coat *Tuileries* had a red wool band set below waist level, and a strip of the wool up the centre front. The silhouette was of a discreet triangle, falling from a narrow shoulderline to a modestly full skirt, approximating to the Eiffel Tower's general silhouette. The coat itself was in black wool.

Domes and cupolas were reflected in panelled skirts. In evening dress it was a full skirted black satin strapless gown, with a decorative band this time, encircling it at thigh level and terminating in a bow in white satin. Cupola dress panels reached up the neck on day gowns, so they were a variation on Worth's princess line. The collection was largely in grey and cinder tones. The lighter range was of rainbow hues, violet and Christmas pink, a lively descendant of Christmas red. The fabrics were chiefly pure wool, or mixed cloth with wool and silk, and tweed. Many satins for evening were laméd, or embroidered and brocaded.

31 **Dior's Tulip Line in model** Jardin Japonais, **summer 1953. The Aschers got the idea for this screen-printed silk from a Chinese water-colour, and called it Blue Bird, but Dior renamed the model 'Japanese Garden'. This afternoon ensemble had a coat, not shown, and this slender dress with the draped effect across the neckline and cap sleeves as the Tulip. Hemlines had lengthened since Dior's Long Line in 1951 (Photograph courtesy of Zika Ascher).**

in 1954, where the line was again the Lily of the Valley, which Dior stated inspired volume for the hat, volume for the bust and volume for the skirt, and evoked three soft rectangles to cover the figure. He wrote: 'The new mode says goodbye to the princess line, and sails towards new adventures. Young, supple and simple, like the flower which incarnates it, the fashion for spring imposes no fetters on women other than what suggests to her her own coquetry.' He deliberately broke the long effect with waists, sashes and belts. Tailored suits, two pieces, blousons and spencers were all grouped together, and all such garments helped to break the long line. The spencers and blousons were often teamed with low cut dresses, to carry them from day to dinner party. The fundamental trend away from volume in coats was continued. The English language does not have the precise vocabulary to equal Dior's statement that *manteau* tended to become *pardessus*. Both words mean overcoat in English, but the first was a full coat, related to mantles, and the latter a narrow coat. Of course in the seventeenth century *manteau* meant a gown. Collars returned in this collection, on the overcoats which had a very tailored sharpness after so many years of fullness.

Short coats were also featured and they tended to have their own sleeves of raglan or dolman type. There were also short jackets, worn with sheath skirts, which sometimes reached below the waist, and had a blouson looseness about them. Day dresses were dominated by the chemise dress or shirtwaister, with a collar and a

33 **Model** Compiègne **in Ascher satin, autumn–
winter 1954. Cupolas had resurfaced in Dior's
winter collections for 1953 and continued into
winter 1954. The fabric and the dress were a
tribute to Worth and the Second Empire, which
used to hold receptions at the Château de
Compiègne. The screen-printed satin decoupé
velvet, was woven with extra satin warps, which
were cut by hand to produce the velvet flowers.
The cut of course is Worth's princess line, with the
panels draped up into the bodice. The colour was
light blue with rose flowers. Zika Ascher
remembers that 38 feet (11.5 metres) were used
for** Compiègne **(Photograph courtesy of Zika
Ascher).**

belted waistline. The skirts were either supplely simple, pleated or full. Typical of this look was *Tour of the World*, in grey flannel flecked with white. It had a blouson type jacket with a shawl collar, and fastened tightly at the waist, whence sprang large pleats. Underneath was a chemise top with two straps at the shoulder, which would convert the ensemble from lunch to dinner dress. It was one of Dior's practical creations, among many which did not seek to be, such as the tailored suit *Ranelagh* in navy blue wool spotted with white. The skirt was so narrow walking was out of the question. Rather it was for posing in. The hip-length jacket had four deep pleats on the front which continued down to the basque, and a belt that passed under them. This suit also had regained a collar. Evening gowns were much slimmer. *Goodnight* in embroidered cotton, had a strapless bust formed of panels and pleats, to create a tiny waist, and a moderately full skirt to the ground. Another in pale blue silk had some folds springing from the waistline which did not however cause the skirt to flare outwards. It had its own spencer type jacket worn very loosely with wide sleeves. Stoles, scarves, and large wraps which Dior termed togas, were common with evening gowns. *Spanish Night* was a very simple gown of embroidered cotton piqué, with a strapless boned bodice, and a skirt whose fullness was only about two metres round the hem. Dior's old bustle effects resurfaced on *Southern Night* in white organza strewn with metal pieces in royal blue. The back of the skirt was folded into a standing frill, reminiscent of 1701–10. The bodice was strapless as were most such items for evening.

The daywear was predominantly coloured Parisian blue, with black, white, grey and lilac as the secondary range. Short evening dresses for cocktails and cabarets were mostly black. Full evening dress had the colours white, blue, lilac, red, pink, and the new petunia. Navy blue returned for the tailored wear. Printed silks continued to be liked by Dior, and he said that shantung was indispensable for its ability to take colours.

Dior had been trying to dispense with the waist with his Empire line hints, and his hip-length sweaters, and in the autumn 1954 he took the full plunge, with his H line, the hipped silhouette. He wrote in the programme, 'The hour H chimes a line entirely different, based on length and the

*34 **Model** Gracieux **in Ascher's Baboushka print, summer 1954. Dior used Ascher's silk organza for both this boutique summer dress and a haute couture ensemble in the salon upstairs. Little Tudor roses are outlined in black upon a rich-rose background. Dior interpreted it in this halter-necked sleeveless summer dress (Photograph courtesy of Zika Ascher).**

35 **Dior dress in Baboushka print, summer 1954. A cocktail ensemble in the salon. The bodice is boned and covered with a draped effect, and has one of Dior's bows at the waist. The skirt is loosely pleated and would blow in the wind. (Photograph courtesy of Zika Ascher).**

36 **Dior H-Line evening dress, Seeberger Frères, April 1955. On most of his H Line models, Dior used two waistlines, one at the hips and another at the natural waist, to temper the extreme effect of his back to the 1920s look. This black velvet evening gown is covered with silver embroidery, with the longest elements at the bust, the hips and below the knee. The elements at the hips are different however, being elongated ovals without the square heads of the others, so that they are given a subtle prominence (Bibliothèque Nationale Paris).**

reduction of the bust. It is on two parallels, forming the letter H, that dresses, suits and coats are constructed.' Thus the blouson and jackets now terminated at the hipline. Fullness now sprang from the hips, in a manner reminiscent of the Twenties. It was a youthful line requiring a slim figure, and it ignored the natural waistline. Seven years after reviving corsets, Dior now turned increasingly to less constrictive clothes. The influence of Captain Molyneux is probable. He always declared that the first question to ask of an idea, is, is it wearable? Dior's blousons, shirtwaisters and chemise dresses were all very wearable, and show him forsaking the extremes of his first collections.

The short evening dress *Priscilla* typified the new style. It had a chemise or vest-like top falling to the hips, where a wide sash and bow emphasised the low waist, and then a flared skirt to just over the knee. It was in a milky coffee satin. Dior did not conceal his beloved waist entirely, for the H-Line bodices did narrow at that point, so that they had a new low waist marked by sashes, and a hint of the old natural waist as well. The short evening gown *Zelie* had a halter neckline in pearl-grey satin, and was buttoned double-breasted with princess seams from below the bust into the hips. It curved in at the natural waistline, but shot out into two wide flares at the hip, although the central panel remained flat. Thus Dior approached his revolutionary look in a conservative manner.

*37 **Dior's A Line, John French, May 1955.** A copy in cotton tweed by Frank Usher London at 27 guineas. The line of the buttons imitates the A, and the Eiffel Tower of Dior's earlier look, demonstrating that both lines are related. It shows Dior's development away from the tight corsets of his first collections towards the waistless dress, which would dominate his last lines (Reproduced by courtesy of Vere French; photograph, The London Darkroom).*

The princess line was also back, for Dior used it on *Grand Dinner*, a black satin dinner gown with a boat neckline, and princess pleats forming a normal waist and full skirt, so there were some alternatives for customers who found the H Line too great a change. Evening jackets were still around for the arrow slender strapless gown *Amadis* had a slender jacket with short sleeves in the same pink satin embroidered with pink spangles. From this it was but a short step to the evening suit, featured in *Zemire*, a silver-grey satin strapless evening gown with a fitted jacket reaching to the hips. It had a fold as a collar – formal collars had again been abandoned in this collection in favour of folded or draped collars.

The severity of the H had offended some customers, as Dior showed when he introduced the line for spring 1955, the A line.

'For the rigour of winter, and the parallelism of the H Line, the silhouette for spring substitutes a freer line, more opened out, which perfectly symbolises the letter A, of construction very close to the H, but based on an inflexibility of two diagonals where the angle is susceptible to a thousand variations.'
It was the H line with the sides tilted inwards, but it retained the low waistline, and was related to the Eiffel Tower look. Molyneux's stress on evolution not revolution now entered Dior's vocabulary and he wrote of the A Line 'In resumé, a sensible evolution, not the revolution of the silhouette in general, whose possibilities have not yet been exhausted.' Clearly Dior still found the H and A exciting, so he continued to try out ideas on those themes.

A major style of the collection were the vest dresses, with the top cut like a sleeveless vest, and teamed with a flared, pleated skirt at the hips, to produce the A silhouette. It could be worn with a short-sleeved jacket by day, be worn bare armed for dinner, and it also had a matching A-Line coat, formed of long panels shaped to flare at the hem in the manner of the princess cut. It had no waist but for sloping pockets at the hip. *Alouette* was the example worn in the collection, in natural shantung silk. Another variation was *Anglomania*, a short-sleeved vest dress, with pleats at the hips, which had a long, waistless jacket to accompany it, which hinted at the old waist by being gathered in loosely, but which ended at hip level. The model *A* was a three-quarter coat, again waistless, worn over a short-sleeved vest dress with a pleated skirt. The line was also applied to the shirtwaister *Alliance*, which had a shirt top to the hips, gently shaped to indicate the whereabouts of the natural waist, but ending with a sash and bow at the hips, and a flared, pleated skirt. This was in sky-blue linen. Differing from the main line was *Adele* in a pale-blue organdie embroidered with roses. This had a short-sleeved, shirtwaister top, clinched into a tight waist at the natural position, and a flared skirt over net petticoats, reaching just over the knee. This model, not the As and Hs, would be copied thousands of times, and become the absolute uniform of teenage girls for the rest of the 1950s. For evenings the vest dress was a pink satin slip to the hips where the skirt was hauled up and draped to anchor on the left hip with a bow. It was pure 1920s: Dior had a great liking for some of the streamlined styles of his youth. There were sleeveless jackets for evening in black cloth edged with black satin, reaching down to the hips, over an arrow slender vest dress below. For restaurant wear it was teamed with a beret worn on the side of the head, like a French *matelot* or onion man.

In April 1955 there was a presentation of Dior gowns in South Africa for the anniversary fund of the National War Memorial Health Foundation. The programme for the event is very informative for it listed all the prices, which the fashion magazines did not. The collection of suits, afternoon dresses, cocktail gowns and evening gowns, with of course a bridal gown, was valued at 50,269,000 francs or £55,000. The most expensive models on show were *Adelaide*, a short evening gown in embroidered white organza, and *Aladin* an embroidered evening coat in lilac surah silk, which both cost £900. A full-length evening gown in embroidered rose satin was £950, and was entitled *Fête à Trianon*. The most expensive Dior fur coat on show was £4,000. Many of the dresses were given South African names: *Cape Town* was a rose pink linen dress and coat at £230; *Durban* was a short evening dress in white lace at £245 with a cotton organdie coat at £375; *East London* was a pale blue linen dress at £185 with a navy-blue coat at £145; *Johannesburg* was a printed-silk evening gown in blue and yellow at £195; *Kimberley* was a short evening gown in navy at £275, with a blue taffeta coat at £150; *Pretoria* was an evening gown in shot faille silk at £185; *Port Elizabeth* was a full-length evening gown in grey satin at £200; *Transvaal* was an embroidered full-length evening gown in white; *Zambesi* was a short evening gown of printed silk in green on white at £245; *South Africa* was a mahogany and grey printed-faille evening gown at £275.[1] There were 73 Dior hats in the presentation, plus Dior furs, Dior shoes, Dior gloves, Dior stockings, and the scents Miss Dior and Diorama, reflecting all the licensed lines the house had established. The A Line was prominent in this collection. The chief colours were burnt brown, black, navy and grey for town suits, and coats; for summer dresses natural shantung, and clear browns; for summer evenings, delicate colours with names recalling the French monarchy, Marie Antoinette blue, pink Rose Bertin, Versailles gold and white, Trianon grey,

38 **Dior evening gown, Seeberger Frères, February 1955. For the conservative customer Dior retained some crinoline gowns, for he continued to love Worth and the Second Empire. This spotted evening gown actually has covered shoulders and cap sleeves, unlike his usual exposure of the neckline, and consists of spotted net over silk. The petticoats were probably in nylon (Bibliothèque Nationale Paris).**

Dauphin green, Queen's Hair blond, and royal red. Dior used some man-made fabrics in this collection: nylon, orlon and fibrane in addition to the tweeds, shantung silks, and organdies. He wrote: 'woollen cloth, for its sculptural qualities, remains the incomparable fabric for the couturier.'

For winter 1955 Dior announced a reaction against low waists, and the evolution towards a new line with a high bust, the Y Line, his third alphabetical concept in a row. It was the Tulip Line reborn, with the bulk placed at the top, and an extremely slim stalk for the remainder of the body. There were also some oriental or Near Eastern elements in the collection with Dior's puffball or harem skirt, and some caftans, turbans, Kalmuk toques and Persian bonnets. The Y silhouette was best seen on the suits and two-pieces. Shoulders were wide, and sloping, with the sleeves often cut in one piece with the jacket bodice, as on the dress and jacket in speckled tweed *Persian Blue*. The dress beneath was very slim with two tabs rising from the hips to button at the high waist point. *Voyager* was a suit with a hip-length jacket without a collar, a narrow dress, and a large scarf which buttoned over the other garments, with the ends crossed over in Dior's old scissor look. The A Line still could be found on the suit *Swift Turn* in grey serge, with a small shawl collar, and a hip-length jacket, where the skirt was sprung in box pleats.

In 1955 the film star Olivia de Havilland married Pierre Galante, wearing a Dior A Line suit with a three-quarter-length jacket over the pleated skirt. There was a Chinese-type tunic on the model *Surprise*, in Sekers black shantung satin, which Dior called a 'camisole à la chinoise', worn over a slender skirt to just below the knee, a reminder of his Vertical look perhaps. The Y Line for evening was a huge bow on a black faille evening coat forming the collar, and the rest of the coat falling in an A silhouette. The H could be seen still in the short evening gown *Havana*, in Chaldean-brown faille, which had a cowl collar, and had a full skirt springing out at the hips. An unknotted sash fell down in front. The princess line continued to be employed, as in the cocktail dress in red faille, which had the pleats starting at the short hemline and continuing up to the bust. *First Evening* in white satin embroidered with grey pearls, was a full skirt, full length evening gown cut in princess line. *Evening in Toledo* in black velvet, with a straight

neckline and long sleeves, was another full-length gown cut on the princess line. *Brilliant Evening* was yet another in pink satin, veiled with blue grey tulle, embroidered with silver spangles. The popular, short, full, flared-skirted shirtwaister was presented with another example, *Romantic Evening*, in sky blue rayon tulle, which had a V neckline and short sleeves, and was decked all over with blue velvet strips and spangles. The colours were dominated by the Near East, with Chaldean brown, Syrian yellow, Persian blue, Turkish green, plus Dior red. For evening the choice was pinks and pale blue, ivory and white.

Dior had sought to lift the waistline with the Y Line, and continued this idea in his spring collection 1956 with the Arrow Line. To lift the figure he made the caraco short jacket a feature of the collection, or as *Harper's Bazaar* put it, he was obsessed with boleros. The wide-shouldered top remained as part of the new silhouette, now applied to the short jackets. Dior said he was dispensing with the princess cut this season, so that all his dresses would have two elements, the short jacket and the dress, and on suits, blouses replaced vest tops. The short jackets had tiny basques, and some none, with shawl collars and tailored collars. The obvious link with his high waists was the Directoire or Empire line, and they were included in the collection. A full-length black satin evening gown, with two shoulder straps, was dramatically decorated with a wide white satin sash which formed a bow at the Empire waist level. It was

39 *From Narrow to Wide: Dior's 'A' line, anon, illustration from* Woman's Journal, *1955. On the left is a linen dress with full skirt, just below knee-length; next to it is a tailor-made suit in shantung silk with hip-length, fitted jacket and wide, pleated skirt. The strapless ball gown, though its skirt is full, recalls the 'Empire' line with its waistband just below the bust.*

From Narrow to Wide

selected by Elsa Shelley
at the Paris collections

HERE is Dior's A line with the uninterrupted length of bodice from narrow shoulder to banded hip, with the lightly fitted waistline. Avoidance of nearly all trimming gives that completely plain look which is this season's chic. You see this new silhouette in the first dress of linen with the spreading skirt, and in the suit where the line is emphasised by a finely pleated skirt. This tailormade is of the fashionable shantung which also makes Dior's guilelessly perfect Empire evening dress.

DIOR

Réproduction Interdite

accompanied by a white shawl in white satin organdie. Black Acrilan was found on the cocktail dresses, along with black mixed cloth of silk and wool from Sekers and Bianchini Ferier.

The Arrow was the three-piece *Paris* in black surah silk with maize yellow spots, which had a slender coat with a tie collar, and three quarter sleeves, a top with a boat neckline and the broad shoulders pleated into the neck, and a narrow skirt.

Dior may have said that he was not using the princess line, but it was still present in *Romance*, a strapless short evening gown in white silk organdie, embroidered with mother-of-pearl-coloured glass pearls and tubular beads. It was fitted to the body, and flared out into a skirt that was supported by net petticoats, and it had no waist seam, so the construction was pure princess line. Some coats were growing voluminous again, after their slimming down, and this would continue in the next collection. *Elle* pointed out that the high waistlines were of two kinds, for evening the true Empire level below the bust, for day lower at the bottom of the ribcage. Black dominated the day wear, with navy in second place, and fewer examples of the browns, beiges and blonds. For cocktail time onwards he used carnation red, pale blue, lively pink, mauve, yellow, green with the clarity of opaline. Some touches of Dior red, Mediterranean blue, strong blue, emerald green, were also added. Tweed was employed less, serges and Cheviot cloth increased in application, along with

40 *Princess Marina Duchess of Kent, Cecil Beaton, 1956. Dior's Arrow line was the principal style for the spring in 1956. This lean line returned the waist to its natural place, but otherwise was cut very narrowly. Here the drapery of the evening gown is controlled and interwoven, and not allowed to flare. Only the stole has that freedom. The princess stands before Lazslo's portrait of her mother Princess Nicholas of Greece (Camera Press Ltd).*

alpacas and mixed silk and wool cloths. Muslin and georgette were increasingly used for evening wear, along with printed silks, the principal pattern being roses. Dior stressed the clear–obscure prints of dark bouquets on black of special manufacture.

He remained with bulk at the top of the figure for his next collection, the Magnet Line for autumn 1956. Shoulders were very rounded, and the sleeves were mounted in a new way. Dior said 'mounted very much to the rear, they sometimes form a true part of the back [panels], rounding the shoulders in the Magnet, without however exaggerating the breadth.' Capes were used to make this rounding of the shoulders even more clear. 'Bulk is back' stated *Harper's Bazaar* for September 1956, and this was seen most particularly in the coats, which were like tents, with very deep armholes down to the elbow. Standing collars were a new feature, and some coats had capes. Scarves continued to be employed to create this upper bulk. Dresses were either the princess cut, or the Dutch cut, emphasizing the hips, with a belt at the normal waist. Hems were 40 centimetres ($15\frac{3}{4}$ inches) from the ground, except for evening wear which reached to the bottom of the calf or to the ground. On some models Dior dropped the hemline to above the ankle, which is what Balenciaga had done in 1953, so clearly he was wondering if this was the new length, and was now trying it out himself. It did not make an impact. Dior was more famous for the shortest hems in Paris, just below the knee, and this was the length all the young copied. The muslins, georgettes and chiffons for evening continued in this collection, in both long and short versions, with Empire waists. The Magnet could be seen in evening jackets, like *Bosphorus*, in night-blue velvet, embroidered with pearls, gold and emerald green studs. The short-sleeved jacket was cut in one, with very curved shoulders set well back, and was

bolero in type. The dress beneath was princess line in cut. A lot of the evening wear was full-skirted as in *Whirlwind*, in pale green silk muslin. It had two shoulder straps and a fitted bodice, over four tiers of muslin frills, draped up and down like waves, reaching to below the knee. It was as wide as a crinoline so net petticoats would have been necessary. *Delphine* was another short crinoline in red faille, sleeveless with a crossed bodice. The skirt on the left was extended up into the sash, with a bow and fringed end as a false continuation in the same fabric. It was intended for dressed afternoon wear. *Quadrille* too was a short crinoline in black velvet with short sleeves, a V neck, and a bow on the ribcage to indicate the high waist, although being cut in the princess line it had a fitted waist as well. *Salzburg* was a full-length, strapless evening gown to the floor, in pink faille from Coudurier, which also possessed the V neckline and the bow at ribcage level, where it held pleats rising from the full skirt. Black was again the dominant shade, with dark grey coming second. Browns were lichen toned this season, from chestnut to greenish. For evening, Dior red, electric pink and magnetic blue were the chief colours.

Spring 1957 was celebrated as the Free Line, when Dior declared he was liberating skirts, hats, length, cut and collars. Of suits he wrote: 'They are neither wide or belted, but screwed to the figure subtly, their skirts expand imperceptibly which gives them a great freedom of allure. They are all accompanied by blouses, generally in muslin, which are knotted freely around the neck.' A lot of the jackets still showed the Magnet silhouette and it is curious to consider that Dior began his first collection by opposing the broad shoulders of the 1940s, but was happy to revive the style in 1956 and 1957. It was a more curved variation of the look, but it still gave women a 'masculine' shoulder-line, in the

41 *Dior short crinoline gown, Seeberger Frères, September 1956. Dior's biggest success in the high street was his short version of the crinoline, which teenagers adopted in Europe, the USA, and Japan. It became the uniform of a generation. He of course only intended it for his rich clientele, as in this brocade version worn with a fur jacket, but the mass market copied it in nylon net. Dior himself was not aware that this sort of market now existed (Bibliothèque Nationale Paris).*

down to the hips, ignoring bust and waists, and in contrast there were still some short jackets with Magnet shoulders. The hips were still stressed on some models in the manner of the H Line, so that the silhouette tapered from the broad shoulders down to the narrow hips and skirts. There was a Saharan element in loose blouses with wide sashes, which reached down to the hips, and Saharan jackets with long basques to the hips. Dresses were two-piece, with sweater and skirt as the typical combination for the collection, with sleeves mostly short or to the elbow. For cocktail time the long hemlines extended to the calf or lower. The black dresses with crinoline skirts would do for cocktails, theatre, cabarets, canasta, informal dinners, and parties. For formal dinners, gala premières, balls, official receptions, it would be the full-skirted, ground-length gowns about which Dior waxed poetic: 'which have a large role in the evocation of the past where the light of candles, the gold of ceiling ornamentation, and the poetry of the night render life and truth.'

There were many short evening gowns, however, like *Blandine* in printed muslin of corn tones, and polychromatic flowers, which had two shoulder straps tying in bows at the neckline, a fitted corsage and a tight waist, with a flared skirt to over the knee. *Lily of the Valley* was featured again on a short evening dress with a strapless bodice, in white organdie. The skirt had nine tiers of frills each trimmed with the flower, and there were four rows of the flower on the corsage. *Trianon* was similar in construction, with a wide skirt of pink silk organdie embroidered with white and pink thread, and silver spangles to form country scenes. The most unconventional model in the collection was *Normandy*, a suit in grey cloth. The tubular jacket, without sleeves, enclosed the top of the body like a piece of metal tubing, so that no movement of the arms was possible.

conventional definition. Reality is more complicated; some women are born with big shoulders, and some men are born as narrow-shouldered as some women, so the conventional terminology is flawed.

On coats, bulk was reduced after the previous season's expansion. They were still loose but less vast than before. Three-quarter versions were featured. The absence of waists and fullness were all part of the 'liberty'. Some jackets were loose

Only a maid could fit it on the wearer, and it shows Dior forgetting Molyneux's strictures that wearability should come first. Light tweeds, stripes, Prince of Wales checks, and spots were common for the suits and dresses. Mixed cloth for town dresses was an alternative. Evening was shantung silks, organdies, georgettes, and muslins. Printed silks for cocktails. Liberty was displayed in a short evening dress of pale-blue silk, a softly draped sheath, strapless, which ended in a train falling from the back to the floor.

Dior went even freer in his last collection, autumn 1957, the Spindle Line. Dior explained: 'Enveloped between two curves, the line owes all its elegance to its elongation, which carries with it, by compensation, a certain shortening of the skirts.' On dresses the Spindle look dispensed with two pieces, blouses and skirts. The waistless sheath, with curved seams at the sides, was a one-piece entity. Dior admitted that tailored garments were the major problem of the season, because applying the spindle to them was fraught with difficulties. The line was imitated for summer frocks, and some examples were still around in 1963, but the impact was more marked in evening wear. *Opium* an evening dress and coat, full length, in pale-grey satin printed with blue and silver, was a long tube, loose over the hips in the spindle cut, and with a narrow skirt. The coat was equally narrow. This did initiate a change in evening dress into the narrower gowns of the early 1960s. *Opium* was bought by Princess Grace

42 **Dior's Free Line, Seeberger Frères, February 1957. The Free Line was expressed in waistless coats as here, cut on a triangular or A-line silhouette. The cocktail dress beneath is embroidered over a short crinoline petticoat. The waist is not liberated apparently, and is still boned into a bare shouldered bodice (Bibliothèque Nationale Paris).**

of Monaco. There were still plenty of short crinolines in the collection for those who loved them, with black taffeta and black velvet as the chief types. Salmon-pink faille featured on *Venezuela*, a short evening crinoline which had a crossover bodice and looked back to Dior's Oblique look by having a gathering of the fabric obliquely set on the right hip. *Sonatine* looked back to the Victorian and Second Empire periods that Dior loved; a short evening dress in black velvet, it was trimmed at the boat neckline by white lace, and had an underpetticoat of white lace appearing at the hem, like the visible petticoats of little girls in the nineteenth century. It was a style he had imitated when at Piguet's, so it was a long-lived theme in his design vocabulary.

Applying the spindle to suits was a problem, so Dior stayed with the Magnet Line and designed the suit *Dior Red*, in red cloth, with curved, sloping Magnet shoulders on the jacket which ended at the waist, without any basques. The skirt was the spindle, being curved out over the hips. *Harper's Bazaar*, in September, melted at Dior's 'divine chiffon dresses'. These were strapless sheaths for evening, which had draped pieces over the shoulder, or from the back, to fall in slanting tiers.[2]

Dior also designed fancy dress, as well as attending masquerade parties. These were usually copied from paintings. Tiepolo was the source for the shepherdess which Dior designed for Baroness de Rothschild, in yellow and caramel shantung with a laced bodice on the jacket, which terminated in pleated basques. The skirt was as wide as a crinoline, and edged with a strip of velvet. It was worn for the ball given by Carlos de Bestegui at the Palazzo Labia, Venice in September 1951. Another disguise was in 1956 for the ball given by the Vicomtesse de Noailles, and it was copied from Manet's *The Bar at the Folies Bergères*, (Courtauld Institute Galleries). The barmaid's black velvet jacket was copied down to the frilly white collar, and her narrow skirt, part of Worth's *cuirass* line, draped and puckered to complete the lean line. For a private ballet performance at a soirée given by Baron and Baronne de Cabrol at the Théâtre Marigny, Dior created a Cardinal Richelieu costume in 1952, from purple velvet with a white cotton surplice and wide 1630s collar. His public theatrical designs are listed in Appendix I.

From plants to architecture Dior had reconstructed women in a great variety of ways in these ten years of his career. He had evolved from the tight-waisted dictator of 1947, to the waistless dress designer of 1957. Some consideration as to what it was actually like to wear his creations may have penetrated his conscious mind, and the concept of comfortability rather than severe elegance above all had gained some ground in his collections during the 1950s.

4

IDEALS AND INFLUENCES

Dior was Anglophile and a Norman, so he acknowledged freely that he was influenced by two English designers in particular: the great Charles Frederick Worth (1825–95) the first grand couturier in the nineteenth century, and from the twentieth century, Captain Edward Molyneux (1891–1974). The latter Dior knew in person, and he attended two of Molyneux's collections before starting his training at Piguet's, and fell in love with Molyneux's clothes.

These dresses had a perfectly sober and clean line, which was a succès fou *in that period between the two wars. Any hint of the over-severe in them was somehow softened and feminized by the subtle Parisian touch.*

Molyneux's design principle was the avoidance of excess, and the simplicity of true sophistication. The fabric and the cut should say all, and he was known for teaching duchesses to give up their vast ropes of pearls for plain, white collars like their maids. While Dior was at Lelong's he worked beside Molyneux's pupil Pierre Balmain, so the influence of Molyneux continued during Dior's training. Dior admired Chanel for her elegant wit, and

the way she had abolished *frou frou* and Edwardian overdressing, but

my preference was for Molyneux. Nothing is ever invented, everything springs from something else. His is certainly the style which has most influenced me.[1]

Dior probably knew Molyneux only slightly before the war, but Balmain could have reintroduced them in 1945 when Molyneux returned to Paris. The influence can be seen in Dior's grey interiors copied from Molyneux. In 1955 Molyneux bought a flower farm in the South of France at Biot, near Antibes, so Dior bought one too, the Colle Noire at Montauroux, where he constructed a large ornamental pool, and grew carnations. He spent his last summer there in 1957 and popped over for lunch with Molyneux. A Nice newspaper declared that the 'Pope of the Mode' was receiving the 'Emperor of Couture'. But they discussed flower growing not clothes. They lunched on Provençal hors-d'oeuvres and duck with orange, and Molyneux promised to visit Dior's flower farm to give him any advice he wanted.

Admiring somebody and trying to imitate their standards is not the same as being that person. Molyneux was a perfectionist, a disciplinarian, and his cut defied copying. He was the master of the British understatement. This is what Dior admired, but he was too much a romantic to apply Molyneux's ideals all the time. Molyneux would never have stunned everybody with the New Look. He showed padded hips and longer skirts in 1946, but would have removed the padded shoulders only gradually, and increased the volume of skirts slowly, from season to season, so that people would grow used to the style evolving. Dior on the other hand had wanted to make a great impact, and of course he had an American publicity officer, so Maison Dior began with some American swagger behind it. Dior aimed for instant success, not the gradual gaining of a clientele.

Dior did achieve some simple elegance in his dresses and suits in the Molyneux manner; *Bar* was a good example in 1947, as was the suit *Favori* in 1950. A slender dress in black wool in 1952, with only the accents of eight buttons, a belt, cuffs, and a tiny bow-collar, was very much in the Molyneux style, but at other times Dior lacked such restraint, and went over the top. *Peruvian*'s mass of black taffeta leaves in 1949 would have made Molyneux shudder. The overuse of embroidery and sequins on *Juno* 1949, where the leaves were encrusted with sequins and spangles, resulted in the loss of lightness and flutter, for the leaves could not stir in movement, but hung down weighed by clutter. The afternoon dress *Vilmorin* was bedecked with three-dimensional daisies, which must have made sitting down uncomfortable. A gala gown in celestial-blue taffeta of 1953 had a drum farthingale with puckered skirts, that left the wearer marooned in the middle.

But in the idolizing air of a couture house, no criticism of the master's designs was allowed. It is significant that Dior paid only one visit to the USA, although it was his biggest customer, for there he was

openly challenged by the press, demanding that he justify his design decisions. Dior did not like this questioning of his creative instincts, and was only too happy to scuttle back to Paris and his couture house, where a flock of motherly ladies was waiting to look after him. Like many a couturier, he was spoilt and protected by his female staff, who had all been conditioned by other couture houses before they joined him. The only question allowed was how to achieve the master's wishes, not to object to their impracticability. Similarly criticism was not tolerated from the fashion press. The reporter who condemned a collection would be barred from entering future shows. Thus Dior was cotton-wooled with adulation, and the only occasions when he might encounter some critical comment was from fellow couturiers like Molyneux and Balmain.

Dior's views were solicited by the press, but not challenged by them. In 1955 he informed his South African admirers on colour, 'Navy blue to me is summer's black. For a certain age, this softened black, which is navy blue, becomes more flattering. Black is sometimes too hard on some women. But remember, navy blue often lacks the "violence of accent", that makes *black* the most elegant colour.'

Accordingly black dominated his day dresses, suits and cocktail gowns. Of grooming he stated:

In France, walking in the street, I frequently deplore the lack of grooming

43 Dior summer dress and coat, Seeberger Frères, February 1957. Lining the coat with the same fabric as the dress was a characteristic of Captain Molyneux in the 1920s and 1930s, so Dior makes this tribute to his contemporary idol. The Free Line coat matches a sleeveless summer dress, which has an easy skirt, and is tied with one of Dior's inevitable bows. The straw hat makes it an ensemble for garden parties, but with a cocktail hat it could double for evening.

I see in French women; their hair, their poorly pressed clothes, their badly shined shoes.

In New York I was over-saturated with the too 'polished' look of American women. Super sophistication is the enemy lurking behind most American women. I like to see individuality and a more natural look. There should be a medium between your fashion personality and reality – it is YOURSELF!

44 **Dior's Oval Line, John French, spring 1951. Dior as copied by London Town, in worsted cloth, cut on the princess line, with the white spencer in piqué cotton, to retail at £10. The Dior original has a spencer in beige shantung over the iron-grey alpaca of the dress. The neckline continues the Horseshoe neck from the previous year. The princess line cut was one of Worth's inventions which Dior used repeatedly (Reproduced by courtesy of Vere French; photograph, The London Darkroom).**

He stressed, 'on looking natural', that a woman should not look like a fashion plate. She shall never look as if she were just leaving her dressmakers. Her personality should dominate fashion and the current mode. Thus a woman should be selective when deciding how far to follow a fashion, and judging how much it would suit her figure, her way of life, and her tastes, which was good advice. Dior admitted he enjoyed seeing his fashions becoming the rage, and admitted that he designed for a special class of women (those who could pay his bills), but phrased it thus:

I know I design for a special class of women, the elegant of the world. But fashion is dedicated to the WOMEN OF THE WORLD, to women in general. There is nothing I would like better than to make every woman look and feel like a duchess. The lower level must always strive to reach a higher level – it is a law of nature.[2]

It is nothing of the sort, and the younger generation would stage a revolt against Parisian couturiers, ultimately telling *them* how to dress. They were not interested in looking like ladies with dressmakers. They preferred to invent their own American uniform, jeans and T-shirts. Now that the USA was the most powerful state in the world its clothing styles would affect Europe increasingly. Dior died too soon in 1957 to appreciate what was going on. He knew that youth was growing in numbers from the post-war baby boom, and he went some way to providing younger styles with his sweater dresses and crinoline shirtwaisters, but his real interest was luxurious creations in silks and satins, where cost was no object.

It was foolish to talk of the rich as being the elegant of the world, for money does not guarantee taste and sophistication. His clients were filmstars like Ava Gardner, Olivia de Havilland, Marlene Dietrich, Jane Russell, Rita Hayworth, actresses like

Madeleine Renaud, Nicole Stephane, and Edwige Feuillère, rich aristocrats, and the wives of magnates in the business world. Royalty as well: Princess Margaret, Princess Marina of Kent, Princess Paul of Yugoslavia, the Comtesse de Paris, and the Duchess of Windsor were all dressed by Dior. Why should the average working lady be expected to elevate her clothing to their level?

Dior was one of the principal reasons why Coco Chanel decided to come out of retirement. To her he was the epitome of the bad, male designer who imposed all sorts of artificial shapes upon women, without ever referring to the fundamental nature of women's bodies. Dior expected women to convert themselves into plants and flowers, figures of eight, scissors and windmills, cupolas and the Eiffel Tower, the H Line, the A Line and the Y Line, the magnets and arrows, ovals, rectangles, foreigners, and anything else which caught his fancy, without ever starting at Chanel's baseline, the fundamental shape of woman. He assumed the right to instruct women in remodelling themselves to suit his fantasies. He loved flowers, so let all women bloom into roses. The picture may be charming, but it does not hold up very well in the real world where the majority of women have to work for a living, and blooming dresses would soon suffer from the blight of travel, weather, children and machines.

France had produced such warriors as Joan of Arc and Margaret of Anjou, and the scientist Marie Curie, but Dior ignored them. Time and time again he wrote that he was trying to make women more alluring, more seductive, more coquettish, so he subscribed only to the old masculine society's view of women, which the Church fully endorsed, that woman could only be Eve, the eternal temptress, who should be judged on her physical assets alone. She was expected to display her naked shoulders, bust and legs to the gaze

45 *Two Dior evening gowns, Seeberger Frères, February 1952. While most of the clothes in the collections for the early Fifties were slimming down, Dior still retained some full-skirted evening gowns, but even here the fullness was restrained. He continued to use mostly light silks for evening, the tulles and organza. Signs of the Oblique still occur in the neckline of the white gown which is open on the left (Bibliothèque Nationale Paris).*

of males who concealed their charms from Adam's apple to big toe. Dior was packaging Eve for male consumption, presenting her as a seductive ornament, in as many ways as he could devise. He only knew two types of women, the professional glamour girls and entertainers, and the rich. Women professors, doctors, writers, administrators, and commandants, did not exist in Dior's world. Dior never spared them a thought, and left it to Jacques Fath to start designing for the ready-to-wear market. From his very first

46 *Dior evening gown, Seeberger Frères, February 1950. Dior revives Worth's tunic line of the 1860s, and abandons satin for evening in favour of silk muslins, organzas and tulle. Worth had used quantities of tulle in his crinoline gowns, so Dior was copying both the fabric and the two tiered tunic skirt. The bodice is boned to provide foundation, and the waistline dips at the back, as seen in Fig. 14 (Bibliothèque Nationale Paris).*

women into strapless bodices on cocktail dresses and evening gowns, with bare arms, regardless of draughts, the climate or mosquitoes. At most he supplied a stole to guard against draughty halls, but that was all. Only a tiny number of his evening gowns had sleeves. Dior presented wide shawl collars on his afternoon dresses, and wide boat necklines, so the exposure began before evening, and it never left his collections.

A number of decorative features occur frequently throughout Dior's work, and of these bows were the most constant. There were bow-tie sleeves on *Aladin* in 1947, and bows fastening a bolero. In 1949 on *Black Swan* a large black velvet bow occupies the centre front of the white satin skirt, just below the waist, and its ends fall like two black panels over the skirt, in dramatic contrast. On *Pisanello*, 1949, a large navy-blue satin bow ornaments the left hip to highlight the windmill flare below it. *Richard Strauss*, 1950, had a similar effect, with a chestnut and yellow bow on the left hip. An evening gown in 1951 of black taffeta, had an overskirt formed by the bow knot of black tulle falling down over it. *Declaration*, 1951, had a knotted effect on the left waist, forming an overskirt in navy starella. A bow and sash preside on *Mexico*, 1951, at bust level, while *Venezuela* had the same items but with the bow ends falling right down to the ground. On a black satin evening gown of 1953, the white satin bow and sash is located just above the knee on the skirt. With the H Line more bows appear at the hip, such as on *Angelica*, 1954, of pink satin, with a bow catching up the skirt to drape on the left hip. On *Priscilla* in the same year, a bow is placed halfway between the centre front and left hip. *Curacao*, also 1954, was more conservative with the bow at the waist, the ends flaring out into an overskirt. A giant bow formed the collar on the black-faille evening coat *Evening at Maxim's* in 1955.

collection in 1947, Dior was aiming at the exclusive rich, never mind the masses with their clothes rationing and shortages. He had not refused to design clothes for the wives of Nazis during the Occupation, nor was he fussy where his post-war clients came from, so long as they could pay his prices. He only presented the sort of woman which that society wanted, attractive wives paraded by rich husbands at evening parties and cocktails, undressed to a degree that no male would dream of exposing himself. After six, Dior put

A narrow bow collar occurred on the coat *Paris* in 1956. On *Blandine* in printed muslin, bows form the shoulder straps in 1956. Despite all the lilies of the valley on the dress of that name, there is still a bow at the waist. A waist bow occurs again with long ends on *Trianon*, in 1957, but is superfluous to this country painted dress. Small black velvet bows ornament *Sonatina* in Dior's last collection, so they never left his design vocabulary.

Pleats are another regular feature. They were essential for the New Look, and could be seen on *Bar, Chérie* and *Corolla* in 1947. They are a feature of the coat *Mystère* in the same year, and formed the skirt of the shirtwaister *Pactolle* in 1949. Pleats are prominent on *Indecision*, 1952, on *Pink Pompom*, 1953, and on the suit *World Tour* in 1954. They feature in Dior's A Line, as the skirts of *Alouette, Alliance* and *Anglomania* in 1955. In the last collection pleats flared on *Whirlwind*; Dior could not do without them.

The influence of Charles Frederick Worth was continual in the crinolines, bustles and the draped effects, which Dior was doing for the cinema while at Lelong's Worth's flat-fronted crinolines of 1864 reappeared on Dior's evening gowns in 1953, and on the wedding dress *Fidelity* in 1949, with the volume pushed round to the the back. In 1956 Dior placed a huge rose bustle on a strapless cocktail dress in pink faille, and bustle effects were prominent in his autumn collection in 1947, so they were a constant element in his design. But here too Dior could lack English discipline. Worth never burdened his dresses with heavy embroidery, or cut them into leaves, quite the contrary, his white evening gowns for the Second Empire court were decorated only with a coloured sash. Dior did restrict himself to similar simple effects sometimes, but at other times he allowed the French tendency to overelaborate to win through. Perhaps one should classify it a Latin

tendency, for *faire figure* and *fare figura*, to make a show, is a common principle of Latin nations. The full circular type of crinoline Worth showed in 1860 was revived for *Adelaide* in 1948, which had a sky-blue satin bust and hip basque, with a very full skirt springing from hip level in tulle. It was accompanied by a coat in either blue satin, or peach satin with the black version of the dress. It was a waistless coat and dipped down at the back towards the train, in exactly the same manner as the crinoline coats of the 1860s. The costume Mrs Reginald Fellowes wore as 'America', at the Bestegui ball in 1951 was a flat-fronted crinoline. Dior's short crinolines appeared on *Allegro*, in 1955, in white taffeta with black spots, and on *Venezuela* in 1957. Wide-sided crinolines, influenced by eighteenth-century paniers but with a nineteenth-century curve, appeared on *Havana*, 1955, and *Zerlina*, 1957. Moderate fullness featured on *Blandine*, a summer dress of polychromatic printed muslin in 1957, and on the black cloth cocktail dress *Quadrille* in 1956, and the black velvet cocktail dress *Promise* of 1957. While Worth never made such short versions of his crinolines, Dior would have been lost without his great predecessor to draw on for ideas. The scale had changed of course. There was no imperial court in Paris in Dior's day, so there were no magnificent scenes of imperial balls at the Tuileries, with hundreds of women in Worth's swept back crinolines, which imparted a sweeping grandeur to the wearers. The attempts by Parisian society to achieve something of past splendour could not match the originals, because the events were fewer and smaller. The whole of the administration did not attend in glorious uniforms, and government ministers no longer threw balls for the season. One can see why Dior sighed for the period, and loved its styles, but the Second Empire had gone, and Dior did not have Worth's opportunity to be supreme in his art. Worth had no rivals; Dior faced Balenciaga, of the severe discipline, genial Balmain carrying on Molyneux's discreet styles, and Jacques Fath who struck out into new areas of design. Worth had a monopoly, Dior had a large share but it was only a portion of the whole of couture. Too many others had come up to try to imitate Worth's success, an impossible dream when the society no longer existed.

Crinoline fullness can be seen throughout all the Dior collections from 1947–57; only the size varied. Slender alternatives appeared in 1948, and such slender lines could be found thereafter up to 1957. A slender line with a wide top manifested itself in the Tulip Line, 1953, the Arrow Line in 1956, and in the Magnet Line of 1956–7, so these were all variations on the same idea. Similarly the Eiffel Tower look, 1953, and the A Line, 1955, were the same idea recycled. Architectural features occur in the pediments of 1950, usually expressed in triangular openings on the chest which fastened obliquely with buttons. Mother Nature and plant life were the inspiration for the Corolla Line and lianas in 1947, for the Tulip Line in 1953, and the Lily-of-the-Valley Line of 1954. Perhaps cyclonic lines and windmills in the wind would relate to nature too, but the Scissors Line remains uncategorized. Lastly came Dior's looser styles in the Free Line and Spindle Line of 1957, which were both variations on the same theme. Thus there was a fair amount of continuity in the Dior collections, although it was less obvious at the time, with different titles being announced every season. The biggest contrast in his design policy was the abolition of bulky shoulders for a sloping line in 1947, but there was a return to top-heavy lines in the Tulip, Arrow and Magnet looks. The imprisonment of the waist in corsets in 1947 was mercifully followed ten years later by loose waisted designs which were the exact opposite. Molyneux's advice must have sunk in gradually. By the end of his life Dior had begun to abandon his earlier extremes.

5

MAISON DIOR, CHRISTIAN AND AFTER

The scale of Maison Dior changed dramatically. From the first opening on 12 February 1947 with three workrooms, two additional workrooms had to be added after the first collection, and by the end of the year the demolition of the stables began to make room for the seven-storey extension, which is still there. The boutique for knick-knacks was on the ground floor, and couture salon on the first floor. In 1948 the hat room was opened. By 1954 Dior said that he had 900 employees, of whom 46 were on the administrative side, and the rest selling and making clothes. In 1955 the figure was put at a thousand staff, in 28 workrooms and five buildings, so Dior was now the biggest couturier in Paris, although still smaller than Worth had been with a staff of 1,200.

Every model gown was filed, with a sketch and number, and its buyers were added to the list, with their nationalities. Thus Dior could tell which models appealed mostly to Americans, South Americans, or the Italians or French. The policy of other lines was begun immediately in 1947, so the advice of Marcel Boussac would have been the catalyst. Christian Dior Perfumes was launched in October 1947 with Miss Dior as the chief scent, and Christian Dior Furs followed that same year. The New York subdivisions started in 1948, doubtless at the encouraging of Harrison Elliot, with, in early October, Christian Dior Perfumes at 730 Fifth Avenue, and on 28 October Christian Dior New York de luxe ready-to-wear at 57th Street and 5th Avenue. A second scent, Diorama, was launched in 1949, when the first licence for Christian Dior stockings was agreed with Julius Kayser & Co in the United States. In 1950 men's accessories were first targeted with Christian Dior Ties and Cravats through Stern, Merrit & Co. of the USA. Christian Dior Fur Inc. opened in New York. A special department was set up at the Paris house for the diffusion of Christian Dior products, and Christian Dior Export was opened in New York to sell the house's lines of hats, gloves, handbags and ties.

The first foreign firm licensed to reproduce Dior models was the Palacio de Heiro in Mexico, which was granted the exclusive right for that country. In 1951 Holt Renfrew & Co. of Canada obtained a similar exclusive reproduction licence for

Canada from the New York branch of Dior. In Cuba El Encanto took out a similar contract. Christian Dior Models Ltd opened in London in 1952, with the exclusive reproduction right for Britain, Ireland and the dominions. Australia's House of Youth made a contract in that year, and so did the Los Gobelinos in Santiago in Chile. Christian Dior Venezuela opened in Caracas in 1953, and Dior himself paid South America a visit at this time. Also in 1953 Christian Dior Shoes, devised by Roger Vivier, was established with Delman as partner. In 1954 a de luxe ready-to-wear shop was opened in London. In 1955 the boutique at Maison Dior was moved to the angle of the rue Francois I, and the range of ready-to-wear shoes made by Charles Jourdan was set up. Dior Perfumes launched into make-up with 22 lipsticks in different shades. On 25 June 1955 the first licence for Christian Dior jewellery was taken up with Henkel & Grosse. Yves Saint Laurent joined the design studio in this year, having been spotted by Dior when a student. In 1956 Dior Perfumes produced the scent Diorissimo.[1]

The suppliers to Maison Dior, the textile houses, the buttonmakers, the beltmakers, the jewellers, the corsetiers, had to take their new collections to Dior at the end of November every year, for him to select items for the following year's presentations. Appointments were booked for 15 minutes, but Zika Ascher admits to holding things up:

When you entered everything was very impressive. Christian Dior was presiding in the middle of a long table surrounded by his entourage, two on his right, three on his left. To the right samples not wanted were pushed – to the left those he liked. Those he liked were registered for a length to be sent on approval – others for a reference sample only. It was fascinating to watch how Dior handled the samples he liked. Just by watching how he handled and cuddled the sample indicated to me how much he liked the different samples.

I used to take with me a large bag in which, in addition to the collection I selected out of the new samples, I also put some rejected colourways, and designs of which I was not sure to be good enough. Mr Dior always insisted that I show him every sample I had in the bag. It took usually over an hour before I was allowed to leave the room.[2]

Zika Ascher also influenced the types of fabrics and patterns used at Dior, starting with cotton in 1950. Cotton was then very much a down-market fabric, used for cheap holiday clothes, and was not used by haute couture houses. Ascher printed some cottons and showed them to Dior who was delighted, and immediately telephoned Boussac and asked him to help Ascher by supplying him with more cotton. Dior used it for a garden party dress, *Romantic*, spring 1950, with a pattern designed by Philippe Julian. Consequently printed cotton became very fashionable during the 1950s, for both summer frocks and evening gowns, often in floral prints. In 1953 Ascher's oriental type printed silk was used in Dior's *Japanese Garden* afternoon dress from the Tulip Line. It incorporated small birds, which French textile designers judged unlucky (possibly because the French shot and ate them) but the dress was featured in many magazines across Europe. Dior would use a fabric in both his boutique and salon collections. He took Ascher's *Baboushka*, a printed silk organza

47 *Dior garden party dress in Ascher's cotton, Maywald, summer 1950. Ascher persuaded Dior to use cotton, which pleased Boussac, and as a result cotton became a principal fabric for day and evening wear in the Fifties. The pattern is by Philippe Julian called 'Romantique', screen printed by Ascher in black on white (Photograph courtesy of Zika Ascher).*

patterned with tiny Tudor roses outlined in fine black on a pink background, and for the boutique Dior used it on *Gracious* a summer frock in 1955, and upstairs in the salon on a cocktail dress with matching coat, and a strapless bodice.

Small scale floral patterns were the norm in the early 1950s but Ascher changed this in 1954 with his large scale rose prints, hitherto restricted to furniture covers. Dior was enraptured by Ascher's large printed roses on pink and blue satin, and was inspired to create his model *Compiègne*, a real salute to Worth and the Second Empire, with 11.5 metres (12½ yards) of satin spread over a crinoline, and draped upwards into a strapless bust in the manner of Worth's princess line, as it had no waistseam. This influenced fashion to follow and large floral patterns became very popular for the rest of the Fifties.

Dior died of a heart attack at Montecatini on 29 October 1957, so he did not see Ascher's mohairs which were a big hit with both French and Italian couture.

The fact that Dior liked to cuddle fabric samples, lends substance to his statement in 1954 that the most important principle he learned in dress design, when at Lelong's, was 'the innate character of material', for that controlled what a couturier could do with it.[3]

After his death Maison Dior, in consultation with Marcel Boussac, appointed from its own studio Yves Saint Laurent to design for the house. His first collection in spring 1958 was a great success. He took the loose theme of Dior's two last presentations in the Free Line and the Spindle Line, and combined them with the silhouette of Dior's A Line, to create his own Trapeze Line, an elongated triangle with no waist at all. He shortened the hem to skim the knee, and the press hailed him as the saver of Dior's tradition. His second collection was less welcomed, for Saint Laurent tried to drop the hems to three inches (8 cm) below the knee. This

was quite modest compared to the ankle lengths tried by Dior in 1956, and Balenciaga's calf length in 1953, but the press said women did not want hems to keep going up and down, so the collection did not sell well. For his autumn collection Saint Laurent played safe with simple pleated skirts to just below the knee, very much akin to some of Dior's own models, so the press made no criticism. Still feeling, perhaps, that he wanted to establish a line of his own, Saint Laurent for the autumn of 1959 introduced his hobble look, with a slender, just over the knee skirt, topped by a modified harem puff skirt above it. Day examples had a tight waist with wide belts, but for evening waistless styles were more common falling loosely to the thigh, where they were tied in to the hobble skirt beneath. It was not a style that could be walked in comfortably, and the press made a huge outcry. Maison Dior decided Saint Laurent would have to go. Marc Bohan was summoned from the London branch. He had joined Piguet's in 1945 when he was 19, spent a couple of years with Molyneux before he closed, and then went to Patou in 1950 from where Dior had recruited him. He was now appointed Artistic Director, a post which he held until 1989. It is significant that he trained at Piguet's like Dior, and under Dior's idol Molyneux, so he is well suited to the house. Jacques Rouët continued as business manager.

Saint Laurent's very last collection for Dior came in spring 1960, and he went all out for a youthful style with his Beat Look, black leather suits and coats, black turtle necked sweaters, and black woolly hats. The maturing ladies of Dior's clientele were horrified. Saint Laurent wanted to turn them into Left Bank students and motorcyclists. It was the last straw. For the autumn collection in 1960 Marc Bohan took over, and played safe, taking the waistless look of Christian Dior's last two collections, which Saint Laurent had continued, but opening out the skirts with box pleating to ease movement. The house and its costumiers blew kisses and heaved a sigh of relief. Maison Dior could continue its old way, or could it? The times were changing dramatically. For the first time there was an enormous, youthful market with money in its pocket. Swinging London began to respond to their needs, and Paris was considered irrelevant. Saint Laurent had been absolutely right, haute couture did need to reflect this youthful style, or else it would be left with a shrinking clientele of elderly ladies whose granddaughters insisted on dressing in 'le style anglais'. The two thousand very rich women who could afford Dior's top prices, were vastly outnumbered by the young. Saint Laurent went off and opened his own house, and continued his Beat Look in his first independent collection in autumn 1960. That house is still working nearly 30 years later, which is three times as long as Christian Dior achieved, so Saint Laurent responded correctly to the change in circumstances. By 1964 Courrèges and Cardin had got the message and started designing for youthful extremes with the space-age look. Maison Dior did not alter its style, so its haute couture began to decline. In 1970 it decided it would have to diversify to survive, and began its Christian Dior menswear line, with the Monsieur Boutique. Marc Bohan designed for it to begin with, and in 1983 M. Dominique Morlotti was appointed as designer for the men's ready-to-wear collection and its accessories. This proved a lifeline, for by 1985 the wholesale volume of Christian Dior menswear and accessories accounted for 40 per cent of the total volume for the whole Christian Dior company. The founder would have been astonished, that almost half of his house was now manufacturing menswear. If he had lived Christian Dior would have felt very bewildered by the changes. To improve the distribution of menswear, franchise shops were opened in 1986 in

Cannes, Nice, Madrid and Geneva.

It was not only Dior who faced changes– so did Boussac Cottons. Man-made fabrics had improved greatly, and made huge inroads into cotton's traditional markets. Retrenchment was necessary so Boussac decided to sell Christian Dior Perfumes, then making about $24,000,000 of which 60 per cent was the scents and 40 per cent make-up. It was purchased by the Moët-Hennessey group who retain it to this day. This proved only a temporary aid, and in 1978 mighty King Cotton crashed. Marcel Boussac, aged 89, had to face the receivers. His group was losing £1,200,000 a month and could no longer pay its wages and social security bills. Many of his textile workers, 6,000 strong in the Vosges, had been working for him for half a century. Everything had to be sold off – Boussac's stud farm at Jardy, his papers *L'Aurore* and *Paris Turf*, his 21 textile companies, and Maison Dior. The old cotton king had been undermined by the loss of the colonial market, the lowering of tariffs against foreign fabrics under Common Market regulations, and the influx of Third-World cheaper stuffs. A textile empire died.[4]

Maison Dior was sought by two American companies, but eventually Agache emerged as the owner and continues to hold the house, as well as financing Christian Lacroix.

The furrier Frédéric Castet had joined Dior in 1953 to make the haute couture fur coats. In 1973 a ready-to-wear fur line was launched using his designs, to be produced by a French manufacturer for sale to Europe, the USA, Canada and Japan. The 100 items are mostly aimed at women, but there are some fur garments for men. In 1984 the new owners of Dior decided to extend this into leather wear, so the Leather Boutique was opened and has a 100 garment collection of which some 40 examples are for men. At the time of writing Maison Dior controls a network of 300 licences for 84 ranges of products in

100 countries around the globe. The highest numbers of licences are for Christian Dior hosiery in 17 countries, men's shirts in 14 countries, and men's ties in 13, which reflects the continuing importance of the masculine element in sales. In 1983 the menswear collection was reproduced under licence in 17 countries, USA, Canada, Australia, Great Britain, Italy, Spain, Germany, Greece, Brazil, Chile, Argentina, Panama, Mexico, Uruguay, and African states including South Africa.[5]

There are 30 boutiques of which seven are in Japan. Dior has never followed Fath in designing ready-to-wear for the mass market. Its ready-to-wear lines are restricted to one or two outlets per country, with Japan as the exception, so the quality that goes with restricted quantity still applies. By 1986, Maison Dior had contracted to 750 employees, in its boutiques, and subsidiaries, and its haute couture had become a minor item in the organization. The combined volume of sales, excluding scents of course, was about £600,000,000 in 1986. The managing director since 20 March 1985 has been M. Bernard Arnault from Agache.

Maison Dior has changed completely, so that the boutiques and licensed lines now form the base of the business. It will hardly come as a surprise if the company eventually decides to close the haute couture section entirely. Nostalgia for the past rarely bothers businessmen. The end will probably come discreetly, allowing it to fade away, as it is doing at present.

A further sign of this move away from haute couture as the principal line in the house came in January 1988, when Marc Bohan announced Dior 2. This new line will be cheaper than that in the boutiques and will sell in selected stores like Harrods. This would have shocked Christian Dior, but his house is going down-market. The prices will be around £200 to £400 for a dress, £400 for a suit, and £500 for a coat. The clothes will be manufactured in Turin by Marco Rivetti's GFT company. For the boutiques in 1988, Bohan said he was aiming for a countrified look, inspired by Dior's beloved rural mill at Milly la Forêt. The colours would be soft, in printed wools, with matching knitwear. Fur trimmed shawls would provide a rural feel. For town Bohan was reviving the New Look for suits with tight waists, but he did not mention corsets. The colours would be bright and the line sharp. For evening he was continuing the flamenco influence.[5]

Some people are confused about Christian Lacroix's connection with Dior. He is financed by the same owner Agache, but this is the sole connection. Lacroix did not train at Dior, and his style would have shocked Christian Dior, Balmain and Molyneux. There is too much theatricality about Lacroix's designs. Wearability and practicality do not appear to exist in his vocabulary.

Dior's heir is Saint Laurent, whom he trained himself. Maison Dior must feel very sorry that it ever told him to leave, for Saint Laurent has matured into a consistently good designer. Once he had got the Beat Look out of his system, Saint Laurent has produced wearable styles year in and year out, and even followed Dior's admiration for Britain by reproducing British blazers and suits. Where he adopts an ethnic pattern, he keeps the dress simple, and in the anarchy of dots, stripes, flowers and checks of 1971, showed his mastery by teaming a spotted blouse, with a flower printed skirt, and a sleeveless jumper bedecked with stripes, where the clothes were extremely simple in cut and line, so that the assemblage of patterns worked. In this area Saint Laurent was more sophisticated than Dior and in a sense he has progressed beyond his teacher. There is a discipline and restraint in Saint Laurent which are admirable, and he learned that from the Dior–Molyneux generation. Significantly he has stated that one must maintain the dignity of clothes. By doing this of course he will maintain the dignity of woman, unlike many other male designers who are still stuck in the old sexual stereotype.

Christian Dior's biggest achievement, assisted by Harrison Eliot and the house staff, was in putting Paris back on the fashion map. After the city had disappeared under the Nazi heel in the summer of 1940, London and New York had become the chief fashion centres, so the press was concentrated on them. Only a trickle of fashion reporters had visited Paris since the liberation, and had been more shocked by the luxury of couture than by its genius. Dior, by gathering all the trends of 1946 into one, set out to make an impact and change the style, and succeeded, especially in the USA. In Europe the New Look could not be copied by ordinary women in Britain, the Netherlands and Germany until 1948. Dior attracted the international headlines, both good and critical, and so notified the world that Paris couture was alive and kicking. In attitude he was a pre-war couturier, designing luxurious clothes for the rich, and not concerning himself with whether the masses could follow him or not, for there had not been a mass market as such in his youth. Fashion had been for the few, and only inferior imitation could be found in the street. The poor wore second- or third-hand clothes. He was unaware of how Britain had given everybody the same quality clothes in the Utility scheme and the Austerity scheme during the war. This meant that people wanted the same standards in their clothes after the war, and were thus very annoyed to behold a New Look which threatened the situation, by being too opulent and expensive for everyone to have a share. The Western world became more democratic after the war, and a Labour government was elected in Britain, so ordinary attitudes had changed. People wanted a new society, and that meant similar clothes for all, but Dior was still

maintaining a pre-war attitude. He was cocooned from the trends, and only produced a very restricted ready-to-wear line for boutiques in capital cities or financial centres. He could see the throngs of youth, and designed some youthful styles for the rich young, but he did not perceive the growth of a juvenile market of unprecedented proportions. If he had lived longer the new world would probably have been beyond his abilities. He died too soon to see the crisis that hit couture in the late 1950s.

Dior did not invent any new techniques of construction of significance, except perhaps in sleeve holes and setting. The Magnet-look sleeve was set right back on the shoulder, and his voluminous coats had sleeves from the elbow only. The statement by the Maison Dior press office that Dior invented the little black dress is without foundation. Black was very fashionable for day wear before the war, and every couture house from Molyneux to Chanel made little black dresses. Sales girls in department stores wore little black dresses before and after the First World War, and the *vendeuses* in Maison Worth had worn black dresses in the nineteenth century. Dior could not invent them: he reused an established form.

In construction Dior would have been lost without Worth's inventions of the princess line, gored skirts, and the bias-cut princess line of 1891, quite apart from the crinolines and bustles. Thus Dior could not be classified with Worth as an inventor. Reusing old styles and techniques was the basis of Dior's design. He gave them a twentieth-century touch, with finer fabrics and man-made textiles. Worth himself had continued the Romantic policy of recreating historical precedents in buildings and costume, so his own designs were based fully on past styles, but he did contribute some novelty and improvement in the construction, which Dior did not. Being an Anglophile Dior does demonstrate

something of the impact of the Protestant clothing ethic upon British dress, which designers like Worth, Redfern, Creed, and Molyneux took to Paris. Many of Dior's black town suits are as plain and Puritan as theirs. Yet Paris was also the capital of Latin excess so that too found its way into Dior's vocabulary, especially in evening gowns where the decoration could destroy the line. Some French *frou frou* was still there, despite Chanel's attempts to oust it. It is in the air of Paris, with all the dramatic statues, the elaborate ornamentation of the public buildings, the swagger of the Garde Republicaine. So perhaps it is inevitable that Dior was influenced. In this aspect he was French.

Thus there were two streams flowing inside Dior's creative instincts, the Norman–British, and the Parisian French. It would take a whole book to trace their influences upon his every design for a dress, but the student of modern attire should be aware of their existence. He could produce simply elegant clothes, and some elaborate concoctions of bad taste, so he lacked the severe discipline of a Captain Molyneux. Zika Ascher was amazed when I told him that Dior's idol was Molyneux. 'But they were completely different types! Dior was a romantic. He did not have Molyneux's control,' Ascher cried. Very true, but Dior put it in print. He could not achieve Molyneux's simplicity every time, but he did sometimes.

Dior cannot be ranked with the first-class creators. He lacked their severe discipline, absolute devotion, resolution

and certainty. He was too unsure of himself, nervous, desperately searching for ideas for lines, as he took plants, the alphabet, architecture, and past fashions to inspire him. He could not evolve like Chanel a standard suit and maintain that through his collections, or imitate Molyneux's three-quarter jackets which stayed in his collections from 1919 to 1950. Dior crucified himself on the idea that he had to seize the headlines twice a year, and it was this sort of pressure which surely must have brought on his heart attack at 52. He was certainly not the genius which a lot of press comment about him has suggested. He made a big impact in the post-war period, but that is something else other than genius, in the creative sense. Paris couture owes him a debt for proclaiming its existence after the occupation. The French government was delighted by the impact of Maison Dior on French haute couture exports, and awarded him the Légion d'Honneur in 1950. For a brief period haute couture was able to carry on in the pre-war manner, making exclusive clothes for a small clientele, and for that Dior was chiefly responsible. His death in 1957 was just at the moment when couture hit its critical stage and realized that it faced a very different future, so one could say that Dior was right for those ten post-war years in giving the impression that nothing had changed, but left the arena when reality was beginning to work through the show.

His company today is still based at 30 avenue Montaigne in Paris, where it houses haute couture, high-class furs or *haute fourrures*, feminine ready-to-wear or *prêt à porter*, shoes, accessories, trinkets and gifts. Also in the same postal district are a ready-to-wear boutique at 12 rue Boissy d'Angles, and an accessories boutique at 3 rue Clément-Marot. But with Christian Dior menswear forming 40 per cent of its sales, it is a very different entity from that which Dior bequeathed in 1957.

48 Christian Dior fitting a toile, Seeberger Frères, c. 1956. The toile in linen was the first trial of a design's practicality. Dior is handling the basque of the jacket, which he liked to be built out to accentuate the hips. As a frustrated architect, structure fascinated him, which is why he liked crinolines so much. The suit would look completely different when made up in tweed or a silk and wool mixture (Bibliothèque Nationale Paris).

NOTES TO THE TEXT

Chapter 1

1 *Cue* magazine, 20 Sept. 1947.
2 Christian Dior, *Christian Dior et Moi*, preface Pierre Gaxotte, Bibliothèque Amiot-Dumont, 1955, p.13.
3 *Harper's Bazaar*, April 1946 and October 1946, p.23.
4 Information from Zika Ascher.

Chapter 2

1 Christian Dior, op.cit., p.35.
2 *Harper's Bazaar*, April 1947, p.27 and *Elle*, March 1947, p.9.
3 Marjorie Becket, 'Paris forgets this is 1947', *Picture Post*, 27 September 1947.
4 *The Daily Telegraph*, 10 February 1947.
5 Information from Peter Hope Lumley.
6 Reproduced from *The Gazette* of the John Lewis Partnership, 1947–8, courtesy of the editor and Mrs L. Poole archivist.
7 Information from Mrs Avril Landsell, Weybridge Museum.
8 Georges Dupeux, *La France de 1945 à 1965*, Librairie Armand Colin, 1969, pp.35–56.
9 *New York Herald Tribune*, European edition, 6–8 August 1947.
10 Christian Dior, op.cit.
11 *New York Herald Tribune*, 15 May 1948.

12 Dior's programmes in French are printed in the catalogue *Hommage à Christian Dior*, ed. Elizabeth Fleury, Museé des Arts de la Mode, Paris, 1987.

Chapter 3

1 *Presentation of Dior Collections in aid of the anniversary fund of the National War Memorial Health Foundation of South Africa*, N.W.M.H.F.S.A., April 1955, pp.7–8 and p.113.
2 *Harper's Bazaar*, September 1957.

Chapter 4

1 E. Rebourdin & A. Chavane, *Christian Dior Talking About Fashion*, trs. anon., Hutchinson, 1954, pp.20–21 and p.30.
2 *Presentation of Dior Collections in aid of the anniversary fund of the National War Memorial Health Foundation of South Africa*, N.W.M.H.F.S.A., April 1955, p.13.

Chapter 5

1 Press Office, Maison Dior: Dior data sheets.
2 Information from Zika Ascher.
3 E. Rebourdin & A. Chavane, op.cit., p.34.
4 Robin Smyth, 'The Fall of the House of Boussac', *The Observer*, 4 June, 1978.
5 Press Office, Maison Dior: Dior data sheets.

SELECT BIBLIOGRAPHY

CHASE, I., *Always in Vogue*, Victor Gollancz, 1954.
CHAVANE, A., and REBOURDIN, E., *Christian Dior Talking about Fashion*, Hutchinson, 1954.
DIOR, C., *Christian Dior et Moi*, preface Pierre Gaxotte, Bibliothèque Amiot-Dumont, Paris, 1955.
EWING, E., History of Twentieth Century Fashion, Batsford, 1974.

FLEURY, E., ed., *Hommage à Christian Dior 1947–57*, Musée des Arts de la Mode, Paris, 1987.
HOWELL, G., *In Vogue: Six Decades of Fashion*, Allen Lane, 1975.
LYNAM, R., ed., *Paris Fashion*, Michael Joseph, 1972.
MENDES, V., and HINCHCLIFFE, F., *Ascher Fabric, Art Fashion*, Victoria and Albert Museum, London, 1987.

DIOR'S FILM AND STAGE DESIGNS INCLUDING STARS DRESSED

THEATRE

Jean Planchon, *Captain Smith*, Théâtre des Mathurins, 22 Dec. 1939, Odette Joyeux.

Sheridan, *L'Ecole de la Médisance*, Théâtre des Mathurins, Feb. 1940, Odette Joyeux.

M. Sauvajon, *Au Petit Bonheur*, Théâtre Gramont, 18 Nov. 1944, Odette Joyeux.

Jean Giraudoux, *L'Apollon de Marsac*, Théâtre de l'Athénée, 1947, Dominique Blanchar.

Roland Petit ballet, *Treize Danses*, Théâtre des Champs-Elysées, 1947, Leslie Caron and Nelly Guillern.

Jean Giraudoux, *Pour Lucrèce*, Théâtre Marigny, 1953, Edwige Feuillère and Madeleine Renaud.

CINEMA

Roland Tual, *Le Lit à Colonnes*, 1942, Odette Joyeux, Mila Parely, and Valentine Teissier.

Claude Autant-Lara, *Lettres d'Amour*, 1943, Odette Joyeux and Simone Renant.

Jean Paulin, *Echec au Roi*, 1944, all the female cast in eighteenth-century dress.

Claude Autant-Lara, *Sylvie et le fantôme*, 1945, Odette Joyeux.

Pierre de Herain, *Pamela ou l'énigme du Temple*, 1945, Claude Saint Cyr and Gisele Casadesus.

René Clair, *Le silence est d'or*, 1946, Dany Robin and Marcelle Derrien.

E. Greville, *Pour une nuit d'amour*, 1946, Odette Joyeux.

Marcel Achard, *Valse de Paris*, 1947, Yvonne Printemps.

Alfred Hitchcock, *Stagefright*, 1949, Marlene Dietrich.

de Melville, after Cocteau, *Les Enfants Terribles*, 1950, Renée Cosima and Nicole Stéphane.

Henry Koster, *No Highway in the Sky*, 1951, Marlene Dietrich.

Roy Baker, *Don't bother to knock*, 1952, Anne Bancroft.

Vittorio de Sica, *Stazione Termini*, 1953, Jennifer Jones.

Anita Loos, *Gentlemen Marry Brunettes*, 1955, Jane Russell and Jeane Crain.

Mark Robson, *The Little Hut*, 1956, Ava Gardner.

Norman Krasna, *The Ambassador's Daughter*, 1956, Olivia de Havilland and Myrna Loy.

SOME COLLECTIONS OF DIOR CLOTHES

UNITED KINGDOM

Bath

Museum of Costume

Evening dress in black satin, 1949, with halter neck and back drapery bustle effect, worn by Dame Margot Fonteyn.

Evening dress in champagne coloured satin, 1949, strapless bodice with asymmetrical drape, and long skirt with asymmetrical bouffant effect on one side, worn by Dame Margot Fonteyn.

Evening dress, *c.* 1950, dull pink satin, with fitted bodice and mandarin collar, elbow-length sleeves, and long skirt.

Evening dress, *c.* 1950, in wild cream silk, with brown velvet cummerbund, strapless bodice veiled by double net, heavily boned. Bolero jacket, and the skirt overlaid with six panels.

Evening dress, 1950, in white taffeta and georgette, worn by French ambassadress Mme Massigli for state visit of French President to UK.

Debussy, 1950, evening dress in blue, with a

detachable train, decked with sequins, worn by Dame Margot Fonteyn.

Day dress, 1951, in blue serge bound with blue silk, presented by Doris Langley Moore.

Cocktail dress, early 1950s, black figured velvet with floral motif, from Christian Dior, London, worn by Mrs Ernestine Carter.

Evening dress, 1953, in gold patterned Egyptian brocade, worn by Mrs Murdoch.

Suit *Daisy*, spring 1947, black cloth, first collection, worn by Dame Margot Fonteyn.

Suit in brown worsted cloth worn by Mrs H. Murdoch, 1952.

Winter coat, 1950, navy gaberdine lined with silk crêpe de Chine, given by Doris Langley Moore.

Coat in fir-green military cloth, 1953, given by Doris Langley Moore.

Hat of burnt tagel straw and ribbon, *c.* 1949, worn by Dame Margot Fonteyn.

Hat of charcoal grey felt, 1949, worn by Dame Margot Fonteyn.

Hat of fancy black straw, *c.* 1950, worn by Mrs Murdoch.

Hat of black velour, early 1950s, worn by Dame Margot Fonteyn.

Hat of plum colour velour, 1950–1, worn by Dame Margot Fonteyn.

Hat of navy and white pedal straw, worn by Dame Margot Fonteyn, early 1950s.

Hat of tagel straw with black velvet bow, 1951, worn by Dame Margot Fonteyn.

Hat of black velour with petersham ribbon, *c.* 1951, worn by Dame Margot Fonteyn.

Hat of brown velvet, 1950s, worn by Mrs Murdoch.

Hat of pampas straw and olive-green veil, 1950s, worn by Mrs Murdoch.

Castle Howard, Yorkshire

Costume Galleries

Evening gown in black corded silk with two bows forming shoulder straps, lined with stiff man-made net. The skirt is cut away at the back to show two panels of pleated tulle which fall in tiers. *c.* 1955, model 12906.

Evening gown, spring 1955, with boat neckline, and elbow-length sleeves, princess-line cut, and consisting of black spotted gauze over light-blue organza. Full skirt and light-blue taffeta sash and bow in front, with long ends, model 53165.

Short evening coat, spring 1957, in pink silk, A-line outline, with large buttons and pockets. Worn by Vivien Leigh, model 86229.

London

Museum of London

Evening dress, spring 1951, of white organza embroidered with straw, brilliants and mother-of-pearl in pattern of flowers and foliage. The bodice has one strap, a wide epaulette embroidered as above. The skirt is moderately full to the ground. Worn by HRH Princess Margaret Rose at her 21st birthday ball. Bodice has eight whalebones, and a basque of elasticated nylon. The waist is 22 inches (56 cm). There are four petticoats of which three hang from the waist, and one from a yoke to the hip. The lining is silk crêpe de Chine. The nylon skirt has discoloured to grey.

Cocktail dress in maroon silk printed with red roses, 1956, Dior London. Shawl-type draped collar fastens on bodice left with two matching roses. Calf-length hemline. Internal corset of black net with eight whalebones. The sleeves are dolman in cut, with gussets under the arm, and zips at the wrists for a tight fit. Stiff net petticoat and nylon taffeta lining.

Victoria and Albert Museum

Miss New York, 1947, day dress in green and white spotted foulard. Tailored collar, bat-wing sleeves, tight waist, straight skirt with handkerchief drapery behind.

Maxim, 1947, black broadcloth dress, with plunging neckline filled with a black bow, and bat-wing sleeves. Full skirt is pleated at centre back. Worn by Mrs David Bruce.

Bar, spring 1947, first collection first model, natural cream jacket, and black wool crêpe skirt, given by Christian Dior.

Hat of straw which accompanied *Bar*.

Jacket, 1947, fine grey wool.

Skirt, 1948, black wool with pink satin flounce.

Jacket, 1948, black silk velvet.

Evening dress, 1950, of black satin, strapless bodice, and flared skirt decked with a black velvet bow, worn by Baroness Antoinette de Ginsbourg.

Suit, 1952, in navy-blue worsted, with belt.

Dress *c.* 1952, of black crêpe heavily pleated, model 15781.

Dress, 1952, of black taffeta.

Evening dress, spring 1953, of printed silk organza by Ducharne, strapless bodice with boned net foundation, and stiffened net and organza petticoats. The Duchess of Windsor wore this model in satin for the Circus Ball, Paris.

Fan advertising Christian Dior, early 1950s, printed paper and wooden sticks.

Evening dress in scarlet silk, 1954.

Skirt toile, 1954.

Evening dress of black faille, *c.* 1955, strapless bodice, full skirt with draped bustle effect at back, worn by Dame Margot Fonteyn. Originally the model had a matching stole.

Evening dress in rose-printed silk, 1956.

Bosphorus, autumn 1956, short evening dress in night-blue velvet, strapless, with the bell-shaped skirt embroidered with gold thread and brilliants, worn by Mrs Stavros Niarchos. The example lacks the bolero jacket.

Evening dress, *c.* 1956, in wild silk with gold thread and brilliants in floral pattern. Sleeveless bodice with round neck, and moderately full skirt gathered in at waist. Worn by Mrs Gilbert Miller.

Evening dress, spring 1957, bright-pink silk faille.

Evening dress, spring 1957, white spotted tulle, with a draped fichu, and bouffant skirt gathered at the waist, worn by Baroness Alain de Rothschild at dinner given by H.M. the Queen at the British Embassy, Paris, March 1957.

Short evening dress, 1957, in eau-de-Nil organza, with draped fichu collar with a rose at

centre front, and a pleated full skirt, worn by Baroness Antoinette de Ginsbourg.

Evening shoes in embroidered pink satin, 1952.

Evening shoes in black tulle over satin, by Roger Vivier for Dior 1954.

Dress, black taffeta, 1952.

'Flying Saucer' hat, 1951, in black plush.

Picture hat in openwork navy cellophane, *c.* 1950.

Hat of cream plush trimmed with petersham ribbon, 1950s.

Hat, low Breton type in black plush, 1950s.

Hat, low Breton type in grey plush, 1950s.

Hat, heart shaped, dark-navy plush, 1950s.

Hat, high crowned, in fine cream straw, 1950s.

Hat, Breton type, natural straw, 1950s.

FRANCE

Paris

Musée des Arts de la Mode
(Collection of the Union Française des Arts du Costume)

Bar, 1947, first collection. Natural shantung jacket with basques, black cloth pleated skirt. Gift of Maison Dior 1959.

Holland, 1947, second collection. Dress and jacket in black cloth, with black leather belt and buttons.

Bonbon, 1947, shirtwaister in black cloth with three large buttons and deeply pleated skirt.

Adelaide, 1948, evening gown in black tulle, with satin bands and spangles.

Adelaide, 1948, evening coat to accompany the above, peach satin trimmed with a band of spangles.

Tropics, 1948, jacket in black cloth embroidered by Rébé with pearls and peacock feathers.

Midnight, 1948, evening coat, black velvet patterned with flowers and black silk braid.

Faubourg Saint Honoré, 1949, black tulle evening gown with bust formed of a huge frill rather like a Christmas cracker, and a skirt of unequal lengths.

Peruvian, 1949, evening gown of black taffeta entirely covered with leaves shapes.

Black Swan, 1950, long evening gown, white satin with a giant bow of black satin below the waist, whose ends form an overskirt.

Unesco, 1949, black serge suit, with two shawl collars, the upper one in black velvet. Darted waist, narrow skirt.

Richard Strauss, 1950, strapless evening gown in chestnut and yellow taffeta, with full-bow effect on the left hip.

Ensemble, 1951, slim black silk afternoon dress with two floating panels flared out at each side.

London, 1950, black dress with pediment feature below the neck, outlined by large buttons, and with rows of buttons on the hips.

Provoking, 1950, afternoon dress, slim, in black cloth with one huge basque sporting a pocket on left hip.

Strapless evening gown, 1951, in black tulle and taffeta, where the sash forms an overskirt on each side by being twisted about the waist.

Mexico, 1951, strapless crinoline evening gown in chestnut tulle, embroidered with half moons in gold thread.

Venezuela, 1951, strapless evening gown in red organza, with red silk bow on the bust with the ends reaching down to the ground.

Rudolph, 1951, suit of grey flannel with pointed neckline fastened obliquely by three buttons. The skirt is missing.

Collarless bolero jacket 1951, with oblique fastening in three buttons placed in a triangle.

Strapless slim evening gown, 1952, in pink organdie embroidered with gold and silver flowers, with matching shawl.

Vilmorin, 1952, afternoon dress in black organza embroidered with daisies with a wide shawl collar formed by a white bertha.

Indecision, 1952, afternoon dress in natural crêpe pleated throughout, the central part of the bodice has the pleating set straight, and the pieces over the ribs are set obliquely.

Saadi, 1953, afternoon dress and coat in grey surah silk printed with little yellow carnations.

Afternoon dress, 1953, lamé in gold and blue, with wide collar, with deep gathers underneath, no sleeves.

May, 1953, strapless evening gown, full skirted, in ivory organza embroidered with green silk flowers and leaves and little grapes in tones of pink and violet.

Pink Pompon, 1953, short dance dress to below the calf in white silk printed with blue and green flowers. Strapless bodice and plain coat.

Long strapless evening gown, 1953, of white lace embroidered with silver sequins and strass, narrow skirt.

Angelique, 1954, pink satin evening gown with two straps and cross-over bodice front, the skirt draped up to the bow on the left hip.

Lark, 1955, three-piece ensemble in natural shantung, coat in A-Line princess cut, with vest top dress with pleated skirt from the hips, and a short-sleeved jacket, hip-length.

Alliance, 1955, summer dress with short sleeves in sky blue linen. A line, with pleated skirt from the hips.

Adele, 1955, short crinoline afternoon dress in blue organdie embroidered with pink bouquets, wide collar, covering the short sleeves.

Andalousia, 1955, Spanish influenced A-Line evening gown with three large frills in the skirt, in multicoloured printed organdie. Sleeveless bodice with deep V neckline.

Cocktail gown, 1955, of red faille silk, cut on princess line, with short crinoline skirt. Short sleeves and V neckline.

Paris, 1956, Arrow Line coat and two-piece dress in black surah silk with print of maize-yellow spots. The top of the dress is wide with a boat neckline then falls like a tunic over the skirt.

Screen, 1956, short evening dress and jacket in black satin, printed with chinese motifs with blue and green. The fitted jacket covers the strapless bodice beneath.

Whirlwind, 1956, short crinoline evening dress of pale green muslin silk. Simple bodice with two straps, over four tiers of wild waves formed by multiple pleating in the skirt.

Festival, 1956, long evening gown of moderate

fullness in white satin embroidered with white mother-of-pearl. Bows form the shoulder straps.

Blandine, 1956, printed muslin in polychromatic flowers and wheat ears, short evening gown, with two bows at the shoulder, and a short crinoline skirt.

Normandy, 1957, grey cloth suit with sleeveless top like a tube fastened by a large button on the left shoulder, narrow skirt.

Zerlina, 1957, black taffeta short evening dress draped throughout, with wide neckline, and shawl collar effect forming the short sleeves.

Venezuela, 1957, salmon-pink silk faille short evening dress, sleeveless, with cross-over bodice. The skirt has an inset panel pleated in at the right hip.

Promise, 1957, black cloth short evening dress with bell-shaped skirt and shawl-effect collar forming the short sleeves.

Cocktail dress, undated, Dior boutique design, in black silk faille with two bows forming the shoulder straps. A long skirt in faille can be added to convert the dress into a ball gown.

Evening wrap, *c.* 1950, pink taffeta, decorated with knots across the bust.

Evening dress and jacket, *c.* 1955, Black lace evening gown with pleated skirt, and a white satin jacket loosely cut.

Musée de la Mode et de Costume – Palais Galliera

Suit *Frimousse*, 1951, in grey flannel. Double-breasted jacket with two rows of buttons, and curved basques with curved pocket slits. Straight skirt.

Suit *Ranelagh*, 1954, in navy-blue cloth. Deeply pleated jacket front has a leather belt weaving through it. Slim skirt.

Southern Night, 1954, strapless evening gown of white organza with royal-blue appliqúe work. Strapless bodice and skirt with standing bustle effect.

First Evening, 1955, white satin evening gown with crinoline skirt sprouting from hip-level, V neckline and no sleeves. Embroidered by Rébé with hanging pearls.

Short evening dress with two straps, and short crinoline skirt. Pale-pink zibeline embroidered by Rébé with pink pearls and mother-of-pearl.

Quadrille, 1956, short evening dress of black velvet, with two pleats from the hem to the bust outlined by black ribbon, and caught with a bow.

Ivory silk afternoon dress, *c.* 1950, of shirtwaister type, with long sleeves. The collar is a tiny standing one, and skirt has alternating panels of pleats and plain.

Musée Christian Dior – Maison Dior

Chérie, spring 1947, navy taffeta dress, sleeveless, with pleated skirt and plain front panel.

Master Key, spring 1947, navy-blue crêpe suit, collarless with pockets on the chest and basques. Narrow skirt, price was 30,000 francs.

Soirée, evening dress, spring 1947. Navy-blue taffeta veiled with black tulle, with two straps, and the skirt in two tiers of pleats, echoing Worth's tunic dress.

African, sleeveless evening dress in panther patterned muslin. Black taffeta sash. The skirt is slim but has a panel trailing off on the right side.

Corolla, spring 1947, the collection's prime example, black woollen dress with tightly fitted bodice, and multi-pleated skirt with a plain central panel.

Doris, afternoon coat in navy blue cloth. Double-breasted, fitted waist, and full skirt with two pockets.

Pompon, spring 1947, black suit, with narrow waist and very curved padded hips, trimmed with tiny pompons at neck, cuffs, jacket front, and hemline.

Diorama, autumn 1947. Black woollen crêpe dress with short sleeves, tight waist, and ample skirt gored in petal-like panels.

Adventure (1987), remake of model of spring 1948, narrow black dress in cloth, buttoned from top to hem, and jacket displaying the Flight Line, with flared-out back panels in chicken's feet yellow.

Jacket, autumn 1948, in night-blue velvet embroidered at the neckline with gold thread, fastened in front by a bow. The neckline is V-shaped at the front and on the shoulders.

Abandon, 1948, late afternoon dress, in black cloth, with shawl collar, which is asymmetric. Wide skirt.

Cocotte, autumn 1948, (copied in 1987). Black and white cloth dress, fitted bodice, narrow skirt to the ankle, with bustle effect in standing frill over the posterior.

Fidelity, autumn 1949 (copied 1987). Wedding dress with white satin bodice and huge white tulle skirt, with a satin sash knotted at the back like a bustle.

Coat. *c.* 1949, black silk faille, fitted coat with full skirt, and a black velvet collar embroidered with jet and black silk, with two velvet panels on the front of the skirt with the same embroidery.

Favourite, autumn 1950 (copied 1987), suit in grey flannel with the Oblique Line in a scarf draped from the right of the neck to the left hip where it flares out in a standing frill.

Secretive, spring 1951 (copied 1987), short spencer jacket with oval neckline, over narrow dress in grey alpaca.

Coat, autumn 1953, fitted coat in black cloth, with two pleats on each shoulder to give the Tulip fullness at the top, V neckline, and a tape from neck to hem holds the buttons.

Curacao, autumn 1954, short evening gown in ivory silk faille, with two straps, buttoned bodice, and a wide skirt with a bow superimposed at the waist like an overskirt.

Amadis, autumn 1954, three-piece evening dress, with a jacket and bodice of pink satin embroidered by Rébé with strass and pink sequins, and a plain narrow skirt to the ground.

Samarkand, autumn 1955, red velvet evening coat, embroidered by Rébé in the same colour, collar and trim of American mink.

Romantic Evening, autumn 1955, short crinoline evening gown in sky-blue rayon tulle spangled and decked with blue velvet ribbons around the neckline and across the skirt.

Voyager, autumn 1955, three-piece in grey herring-bone cloth, with a narrow dress with short sleeves and a panel of buttons in two rows down the front a narrow jacket to the hips, double-breasted, and a large shawl with two rows of buttons to match.

Bosphorus, autumn 1956, cocktail dress and jacket, the dress has two straps and a princess-line cut skirt in night-blue velvet embroidered with pearls, gold thread, and emerald green studs; the bolero jacket is plain with short sleeves.

Salzburg, autumn 1956, evening gown of pink silk faille, strapless bodice with V neckline caught by a bow, which also gathered in the folds of the skirt.

UNITED STATES OF AMERICA

Boston

Museum of Fine Arts

Evening dress, 1956, strapless bodice, and ground-length skirt, in rose patterned white silk. Matching stole.

Evening dress, 1956, black Chantilly lace with floral motif, strapless bodice, long skirt, matching stole.

Chicago

Chicago Historical Society

Suit, 1947, black cloth, with jacket with notched collar, single-breasted, long sleeves, padded basques. Sheath skirt to mid calf with pocket on either side of central panel. Worn by Mrs Edward Byron Smith at St. Luke's Fashion Show, 1947, in Chicago.

Suit, 1948, grey cloth with cowl neckline, long sleeves. Straight skirt with slash side pockets and buttons down the front.

Dress, 1949, Dior Boutique New York, grège pleated cloth. Plain bodice with V neckline, pleated skirt. Worn by Mrs William Englehaupt.

Dress, 1948, black cloth, with collarless fitted bodice, and very full pleated skirt. Worn by Mrs R. Kennedy Gilchrist.

Suit, 1948, brown cloth consisting of jacket, blouse, scarf and skirt. Worn by Mrs Ruth Page Fisher.

Evening dress, 1948, strapless black silk taffeta, with full skirt with draped overskirt, worn by Mrs Sanger P. Robinson.

Evening dress, 1949, in black slipper satin and black velvet, worn at a dinner party in her husband's honour, by Mrs Anna Morris Fishbein.

Suit, 1949, navy-blue cloth lined with navy-blue silk. Hip-length jacket with tight waist and padded hips, straight skirt fastened by zip at back. Two slash pockets. Purchased for $450 at Maison Dior by Mrs Florence Kuttner.

Evening dress, 1949, off-white silk tulle, trimmed with off-white satin. Strapless bodice, with heartshape neckline, and very full skirt of multiple layers of tulle, over boned paniers. A length of off-white satin formed a cummerbund, then looped at centre front, and draped round to the back to form a bustle effect. Worn by Jeanne Brucker to Passavant Hospital Cotillion, 1949. Dior for Marshall Field & Co.

Evening gown, 1950, black lace over black faille, painted with tiny red, green and gold sprays. Sleeveless bodice, square neckline, full-length skirt.

Evening gown, 1951, black taffeta, accordion pleated. Plain black taffeta straps. Skirt had black taffeta petticoat now missing.

Suit, 1951, navy-blue crêpe wool, hip-length jacket, with padded shoulders, fitted waist, and curved basques with curved pockets. Separate white piqué collar buttons on. Wrap-over skirt with diagonal front flap. Worn by Mrs Maxine Wishnick.

Suit, 1951, black cloth with black satin lapels, tight waist, narrow skirt with slit pockets, worn by Mrs Hammon Chaffetz.

Evening gown, Christian Dior London, 1952, white satin embroidered with brilliant-white sequins. Strapless bodice, full skirt.

Evening suit, c. 1953–7, in red and black silk print, consisting of a blouse, over-blouse, jacket, belt and skirt. There is a matching handbag with rose pattern. The ensemble was worn by the ballerina Ruth Page.

Evening dress, c. 1953, velvet brocaded satin with fuchsia pattern and cut-velvet roses. Worn by Ruth Page, Mrs Thomas Hart Fisher.

Suit, 1950s, in black and white tweed, lined with white silk. Shawl collar on jacket, three buttons centre front. Sheath skirt lined with white silk crêpe. There is also a long green crêpe scarf. Worn by Mrs Charles Chaplin.

Blouse, 1950s, in red chiffon printed with navy-blue squares. Darts at waist and shoulder. Full sleeves gathered into cuffs. Worn by Mrs Charles Chaplin.

Dress, c. 1953, in black wool, closely-fitted bodice and lower waistline, high neckline, short kimono sleeves with triangular gussets underarm. Pleated skirt from the hips. Worn by Mrs Albert Newman.

Evening coat, 1953, in green silk faille, with turn down collar and three-quarter-length sleeves. Belt starts at each side and goes round to the back only, where it is fastened with a button. Worn by Mrs William Englehaupt.

Evening dress, 1953, strapless white net, embroidered with circles of silver sequins and rhinestones. Worn by Mrs Thomas Hart Fisher.

Evening dress, 1953, of black net trimmed with black lace ruffles. Off-the-shoulder shawl collar, long skirt with net petticoat. Worn by Mrs Thomas Hart Fisher.

Evening stole, and evening dress, 1953, of brown, black and white floral silk. Fitted bodice with oval neckline and two straps. Full-length skirt, net petticoat and matching stole. Worn by Mrs Thomas Hart Fisher.

Short evening gown and jacket, 1953. Jacket of black satin printed with blue, red and yellow Chinese motifs, over matching dress with two straps forming a square neckline. The jacket is bolero in length with three jet buttons. Worn by Mrs Thomas Hart Fisher.

Evening dress and jacket, spring 1953, in dark-brown shantung silk. The bolero jacket is collarless and has short sleeves. The dress had two shoulder straps. Worn by Mrs Thomas Hart Fisher.

Evening dress, spring 1953, in black silk organza, sleeveless with low bateau neckline, and full skirt. Worn by Mrs Thomas Hart Fisher.

Three-piece suit, 1953, in black serge, the jacket is collarless with V neckline, and straight sleeves. Straight skirt. Cape lined with leopard print silk. Worn by Mrs Thomas Hart Fisher.

Cocktail suit, 1953, in dark-blue cloth, the jacket has V neckline and three-quarter-length sleeves over a strapped bodice and straight skirt. Worn by Mrs Thomas Hart Fisher.

Coat c. 1955, Christian Dior New York, black wool with wide Peter Pan collar and three-quarter-length sleeves. Black woollen belt with leather backing. Worn by Mrs Grant Wilson.

Coat dress, 1955, in black broadcloth, slit up each side to the armhole to reveal broadcloth panels. Worn by Mrs Howard Linn.

Evening dress, 1955, *Mystery*, in black silk crêpe, with two shoulder straps and fitted bodice, with draped back panel bustle effect. Worn by Mrs Howard Linn.

Sack gown, 1955, Christian Dior New York, in black shantung, without waist or belt. Six inverted pleats at the hemline, trimmed with black shantung bows. Worn by Mrs Charles Healy.

Suit, 1955, in brown mohair, with tailored jacket, and two skirts, one pleated and one straight. Worn by Joan Mrs William Geering.

Evening dress, c. 1955, in heavy corded gold silk moiré, with strapless bodice and full skirt, plus matching stole. Worn by Mrs Robert Graff.

Short evening gown, c. 1955, in white silk faille called 'American Beauty'. Bateau neckline, and knee-length skirt. Worn by Mrs Thomas Hart Fisher.

Evening dress, c. 1955, in black silk taffeta. Fitted bodice with shallow square neckline, with hip-level waist, whence a box-pleated skirt with asymmetrical hem springs. Lined with sheer black silk. Worn by Maria Tallchief, Mrs Henry Paschen Jnr.

Afternoon dress, 1956, in navy-blue serge with low, square neckline and cap sleeves, high waistline, and belt, with a loop from the skirt to the belt. White straw hat with trim of white silk gauze petals. Dior shoes of clear plastic and navy-blue satin. Worn by Mrs Gardner Stern at her son's wedding, March 1956.

Evening dress, 1956, in brown net. Bodice is solid with gold sequin embroidery, and full skirt has half moons of sequins in graduating size from waist. Worn by Mrs Kennedy Gilchrist.

Dress, 1956, Christian Dior New York, beige and brown flowered cotton, with white nylon net crinoline petticoat, matching belt. Worn by Mrs Otto Madlener.

Coat, c. 1956, in heavy black wool. Barrel-shaped, with wrap-over front and wide sleeves. Inside four-inch-wide ties begin above waist and fasten at centre front, to steady the coat. Black silk faille lining. Worn by Mrs Albert Newman.

Evening dress, 1957, in black velvet, fitted bodice with low round neckline outlined with puffed velvet, and puffed cap sleeves. Straight skirt. Worn by Mrs Thomas Hart Fisher.

Evening dress and stole, 1957, in white silk printed with navy-blue polka dots. Shoulder straps of navy-blue grosgrain. Navy-blue silk flower on front of bodice. Worn by Mrs Lucy Howard Linn.

Evening dress, 1957, in black taffeta printed with large roses in red and green. Fitted bodice with fitted skirt, tapering towards hem, where it is lifted up on the left side and gathered to form drapery, where are attached wide panels to form a short train on the right side. Bodice is boned and lined with stiff tulle. Worn by Mrs Albert Newman.

Hat, c. 1950, brown felt without brim, with ribbon of powder-blue grosgrain. Worn by Mrs Thomas Hart Fisher.

Toque hat, c. 1950, in robin's-egg-blue velvet. Worn by Mrs Thomas Hart Fisher.

Hat, c. 1950, navy-blue straw, sub-divided into wedges by navy-blue grosgrain bands, navy chin strap and hat pin. Bought for $40 at Bergdorf Goodman, New York, worn by Mrs Tomlinson.

Hat, c. 1950, in black velvet, stiff oval covered with black velvet drapery, with black velvet braid hanging down behind, elastic chinstrap. Worn by Ruth Page, Mrs Thomas Hart Fisher.

Hat, c. 1953, brimless dark-blue felt, with wine satin ribbon trimmings, and rhinestone bow and pin attached. Worn by Mrs Thomas Hart Fisher.

Hat, c. 1953, brimless, back tied, in black silk faille. Worn by Mrs Thomas Hart Fisher.

Hat, c. 1953, in grey pleated velvet, and black pleated satin. Worn by Mrs Thomas Hart Fisher.

Hat, 1953, brimless in black velvet with bow at the back. Worn by Mrs Thomas Hart Fisher.

Hat, 1953, white straw with wide brim, and draped with white dotted, scalloped, chiffon. Worn by Mrs Dorothy Englehaupt.

Hat, 1955–6, Christian Dior New York, brimless, red velvet with red dyed fur trimming. Worn by Mrs Robert Graff.

Evening shoes, 1957, in chartreuse satin, with high heels and round toes. Worn by Mrs Howard Linn, with her evening dress above.

Cincinnati

Cincinnati Art Museum

Fitted evening suit, c. 1953–7, black lace over white satin.

Strapless evening dress in black lace, over layers of light pink tulle, ground length, with black velvet sash, autumn 1956.

Strapless evening gown, c. 1956, in black-silk satin with slight bustle effect at rear.

Cocktail dress, c. 1949, calf-length in knife-pleated black silk.

Afternoon dress, 1948, with long sleeves, in dark-blue silk printed with large grey circles, matching belt, and two big pockets on each hip.

Cocktail dress, c. 1956, of pleated, floral-print silk chiffon, with full skirt to ground, and cummerbund in cranberry and pink silk taffeta.

Kent State University

Silverman Rodgers Collection

Evening gown *Venus*, autumn 1949, in pink tulle embroidered by Rébé, strapless bodice, and huge leaf shapes, cascading down the back into a train. Each shape is covered with feathers, strass and sequins in pink mother-of-pearl. A grey version of the dress is at the Metropolitan Museum, New York and a pink version in the De Young Museum of Art, San Francisco.

Short evening dress, spring 1956, strapless bodice, into which a full skirt is pleated, all of silk muslin embroidered with silver sequins, and with pink, green and silver thread, in a pattern of flowers, leaves and peacocks.

New York

Brooklyn Museum

Coat *New York*, autumn 1950, in black cloth, fitted waist and flared skirt, no collar, but an oblique scarf-collar is buttoned on.

Suit *Virevolte*, 1955, consisting of a dress and jacket in grey and white serge lined with silk. The dress has cap sleeves, a draped collar, and a semi-full skirt with pleats from waist to hem at intervals with plain panels. The jacket is hip-length and slim, with a small shawl collar, long sleeves and three buttons.

Suit and blouse, 1955, in red cloth, the blouse black embroidered round the neck with ribbons and pearls. The jacket is in the Y Line, with wide shoulders, and the skirt tapers towards the hem.

Afternoon dress, autumn 1949, in pale-green silk brocaded with silver, short sleeves, shawl collar crossing over to the right waist, and very full skirt to below the knee.

Fashion Institute of Technology

Cocktail dress, *Bertha*, autumn 1952, in black silk, with an off-the-shoulder collar of gathered, padded frill, which also forms the cap sleeves. Fitted bodice, full skirt to the calf.

Coat *Award*, 1952, in black cloth, with an asymmetrical fastening, no collar, and the buttons set as one, then two down. Full skirt with slit pockets with two buttons each.

Coat *Tuileries*, autumn 1953, waistless in black cloth, decorated overall by a cross shape in red cloth, with the horizontal bar at the hips.

Short evening gown *Zelie*, autumn 1954, in pearl-grey satin with halter neck, which can unbutton at the bottom to convert into a shawl-like halter neck, for the front of the dress is double breasted. H-Line fullness spreads out at hip level.

Short evening dress *Havana*, 1955, in brown silk faille, with draped collar, and lean bodice, with a short crinoline skirt sprouting at hip level. Two panels descend from the bodice sides to the hem.

Suit *Persian Blue*, tweed in slate tone, autumn 1955. Slender jacket to the hip, over dress with skirt tapering to a narrow hem in the Y Line. A self belt on the dress rises to form a V at centre front.

Trouser suit, c. 1955, with a strapless bodice buttoned in front, and trousers pleated at the hip, in raspberry-red velvet, probably for entertaining at home.

Metropolitan Museum of Art – Costume Institute

Coat *Mystère*, autumn 1947, black cloth, ankle-length, full skirt, with eucalyptus-green pleated taffeta collar and underskirt.

Aladin, autumn 1947, champagne satin afternoon dress, with V neckline and no collar, with short sleeves held by bows, and a full skirt to near ankle.

Drag afternoon dress, spring 1948, navy-blue cloth woven with mohair, fitted bodice, small collar, tight sleeves to cuffs, full skirt hitched at the hips into folds.

Afternoon dress, spring 1948, showing Zig Zag Line, in black silk. The buttoned bodice has long basques turned back upon themselves to produce Z hems. Plain skirt to ankle.

Coat, 1948, black cloth with slate-blue small shawl collar and cuffs. Hem below the knee.

Dali, cocktail dress, autumn 1949, halter neck, black satin brocaded with gold and bronze leaves. Tight belt in same fabric. Full skirt to the calf.

Windmill in the Wind, autumn 1949, cocktail dress with strapless inner bodice and skirt in black flannel. Wide-cut over-bodice leaves chest bare from shoulder to shoulder, in black moiré, and moiré panels stand out over the narrow skirt, in an echo of windmill arms.

Pisanello, autumn 1949, cocktail dress in navy velvet and satin. Two straps and plain bodice, skirt with large panels sprays out from bow at the hip in windmill effect.

Pactole, autumn 1949, shirtwaister in gold cloth, with small standing collar, long sleeves and panelled skirt with pleats spreading out at hip level.

Trumpet, spring 1950, afternoon dress, in black and white cloth, tight, with the bodice opening on the right side and shoulder, where it is outlined by buttons. Suit has similar right opening with buttons, and narrows to hem where kick pleats are inserted.

Child's bridesmaid dress, long and straight with satin sash as the high waist, autumn 1951. Eggshell-yellow satin, covered in glass pearls, crystal, strass and silk thread.

Fine Party, spring 1951, cocktail dress, in natural ivory shantung, wide neckline, formed by shawl collar set to shoulders, and crossing to fasten at left waist. Pleated skirt to calf. Worn with black net hat and black gloves.

Cicada, autumn 1952, short evening dress, tight bodice, slit neck, long sleeves and long basques, over-calf-length paniered skirt.

Garden party dress, spring 1953, white cotton organdie, embroidered with redcurrants, and artificial glass redcurrants. Bare shoulders and sleeveless bodice, with a bertha in same fabric, covering the upper arm. Full skirt in short crinoline style.

Mexico, spring 1953, evening dress, white silk muslin, printed with concentric festoons of grey spots. Boat neckline, and cap sleeves, over two-tiered skirt, where the lower skirt reaches the ground, and the upper curves upwards from the right to calf length at the left.

Caracas, spring 1953, silk muslin printed with large red flowers and green leaves. Wide neckline, short balloon-type cap sleeves and full skirt to the floor.

Wedding dress, spring 1953, ivory satin, with scalloped neckline, short sleeves, full skirt in panels, embroidered in silver and strass on the bodice down to the knee.

Short evening dress and coat, autumn 1953, with straight dress of satin completely embroidered with opalescent white sequins, V neckline. Straight coat in same fabric and embroidery with three-quarter-length sleeves.

Priscilla, autumn 1954, milky-coffee-coloured satin, short evening dress, with long sleeveless bodice to the hips, tapered in at waist, in the H Line, two shoulder straps and full skirt over short crinoline from the hips where a large bow decorates the left hip.

Philadelphia

Museum of Art

Dress, 1951, heavy gold, black and peacock-blue satin, off-the-shoulder neckline, cap sleeves, fitted bodice, full pleated skirt.

Evening dress, autumn 1957, in white tulle embroidered with crystals and tiny silver sequins, strapless bodice.

Jacket, c. 1950, dark-grey cloth, double-breasted, lined with grey taffeta. Flare-cut in line, with dropped shoulder.

Skirt, 1957, in black lace net stitched on to cotton, and printed with large roses and leaves. Lined with two layers of black cotton gauze.

Blouse, 1957, in knitted black silk, V neck, edged with silk tassel fringe.

Sweater, c. 1955, knitted purple silk, with V neck, edged with matching grosgrain ribbon. Short sleeves and ribbed waist. Matching cardigan with grosgrain ribbon down centre front.

Dress and jacket, c. 1957, pale-green cloth. Jacket has circular collar, short sleeves, fitted bodice and basque skirts. Skirt is pleated and attaches to jacket by press studs.

Short evening dress, c. 1957, in blue and white checked cotton. Camisole top with two wide straps, pleated skirt, and triangular shawl with pleated ruffle, lined with white cotton. Christian Dior Boutique.

Evening coat, c. 1950, in gold satin patterned with small black and rust daisies. Black-fox collar and cuffs.

Cocktail dress, 1947, iced-pink silk satin, V neck, the bodice and collar are cut in one. Raglan sleeves. Deep slash pockets on the shoulders. Full skirt trimmed with horizontal stitched bands, over horsehair and white silk gauze lining.

Suit, 1954, navy-blue wool crêpe. Loose jacket has diagonal front panels, which curve at the bottom into the side seam. Raglan sleeves with inset gussets under the arm. Navy taffeta lining. Straight skirt lined with black cotton.

Evening dress, 1950, raspberry-pink machine lace, with strapless bodice, boned, with scalloped edge. Full skirt pleated into waist, lined with pale-pink taffeta and supported by net underskirt.

Cocktail dress, 1950, in light-blue and lavender silk crêpe. One-sleeved bodice in the asymmetrical line, cowl neckline, which incorporates a short sleeve. Sheath skirt with pleat at right back. A boned peplum extends from the bodice down into the skirt.

Evening dress, 1952, black net encrusted with shirred black velvet ribbons and black spangles. Strapless bodice, boned, and full skirt draped with matching streamers from right waist to back left hem. Black leather belt. Black satin flared petticoat.

Suit, c. 1953, pepper-and-salt tweed, the jacket has a notched collar and long sleeves with buttoned cuffs. The basques flare out and hold the pockets. Straight skirt with diagonal pleats at left.

Evening dress, 1950, in dark-yellow and blue silk faille. Short kimono sleeves, and V neck, outlined by padded overpanel in V shape. Gored, flared skirt with double layers of black net beneath.

Dress, 1952, black cloth, flat collar with triangular pediment neckline, fitted bodice, elbow-length sleeves with cuffs, plain skirt.

Suit, c. 1951–2, in blue and white tweed, V-neck jacket with saddle shoulder, and long-cuffed sleeves. Double-breasted front, cut away at the bottom. Sheath skirt, with kick pleats at left side. White silk lining.

Afternoon dress, 1954, black silk crêpe, sleeveless bodice, fitted, V neck with draped overpanel. Sheath skirt, lined with black silk.

Evening coat, 1948, in navy-blue silk faille, with black velvet collar and cuffs, lined with navy silk.

Rhode Island

Rhode Island School of Art – Museum of Art

Evening gown, 1953, in black Bianchini satin. Strapless bodice, fitted, and boned, decked with narrow band of white satin. Full skirt to the ground princess cut, striped with one satin band in white, rising to a flat bow at centre front knee level.

Spanish Night, 1954, evening dress, with strapless bodice with curved top dipping to a V at centre front, in cotton piqué, embroidered with one row on the bodice and three on the skirt, in blue waves and stars. Full-length skirt restrained in fullness.

San Francisco

Fine Arts Museum

Weathercock, autumn 1948, calf-length evening dress in black velvet and taffeta. Velvet strapless bodice with pointed front. Full skirt in taffeta lined with horsehair, in very deep, superimposed folds.

Juno, autumn 1949, evening dress, strapless bodice, boned, in grey-blue tulle, embroidered by Rébé in blue spangles. Full skirt echoing Worth's flat-fronted crinolines of 1864, but cut into huge round-edged leaves, in a cluttered effect.

Flowered Evening, 1955, evening dress in white ivory satin, embroidered with stars, thread and flakes in gold, silver and blue. Short sleeves, and moderately full skirt to the ground. Crossover feature on bodice, and huge sash falling as panels down the skirt.

Appendix III

DIOR'S LINES

1947	spring—summer	Corolla and Figure of Eight.
	autumn—winter	Corolla and Back of Paris.
1948	spring—summer	Zig Zag and Flight.
	autumn—winter	Winged Line and Cyclonic Line.
1949	spring—summer	Illusion and Foreign Lines.
	autumn—winter	Scissor and Windmill Lines.
1950	spring—summer	Vertical Line.
	autumn—winter	Oblique, Interlaced and Lily-of-the-Valley Lines.
1951	spring—summer	Oval Line.
	autumn—winter	Long Line.
1952	spring—summer	Sinuous Line.
	autumn—winter	Profiled Line.
1953	spring—summer	Tulip Line.
	autumn—winter	Living Line.
1954	spring—summer	Lily-of-the-Valley Line.
	autumn—winter	H Line.
1955	spring—summer	A Line.
	autumn—winter	Y Line.
1956	spring—summer	Arrow Line.
	autumn—winter	Magnet Line.
1957	spring—summer	Free Line.
	autumn—winter	Spindle Line.

DIOR'S SUPPLIERS

England	Ascher Silks
	Seker Silks and rayons
France	Bianchini Ferier
	Bodin
	Boussac Cottons
	Coudurier
	Ducharne
	Dormeil
	Garigue
	Racine
	Prud'homme
	Rodier
Switzerland	Abraham of Zurich.

CHRONOLOGY

1905   Born 21 January at Granville Normandy.

1910   Family move to Paris.

1916-23   Dior at Gerson School Paris.

1923-6   Takes B.Sc at School of Political Science.

1927   National service in French army.

1928-32   Runs modern art gallery with Jacques Bonjean.

1931   Visits Russia to study architecture.

1934   February, ill with tuberculosis.

1935-8   Starts selling designs to couture houses in Paris.

1938   Autumn, joins Robert Piguet's couture house.

1939   Called up into army.

1940   Demobbed, joins father on farm at Callian, Provence.

1941   Summoned to Paris to join Lucien Lelong couture house.

1946   Foundation of Christian Dior Company 8 October, leaves Lelong 16 December.

1947   12 February, first Dior collection. September, Dior visits USA to receive Nieman Marcus Oscar for Fashion.

1948   Dior Perfumes founded. Christian Dior New York opens in 57th St, 5th Avenue.

1950   Private Dior show for Queen Elizabeth and Princess Margaret at French Embassy, London. French government awards Dior the Légion d'Honneur.

1952   Foundation of Christian Dior Models, London.

1953   Dior visits South America, opens boutique in Venezuela.

1954   Dior show at Blenheim Palace, Oxfordshire for Princess Margaret.

1955   Dior speaks at conference on the 'Aesthetics of Fashion' at the University of the Sorbonne, Paris, 3 August. Yves St Laurent joins Dior studio.

1956   Dior publishes his memoirs.

1957   Death at Montecatini, 24 October, buried at Callian, Provence. St Laurent appointed designer at Maison Dior.

1960   Spring, St Laurent's last show at Dior the Beat Look, replaced by Marc Bohan.

1970   Opening of Christian Dior menswear.

1988   Bohan launches Dior 2 line to sell in better department stores.

1989   40% of Maison Dior's business in menswear. Marc Bohan replaced by Gianfranco Ferre.

INDEX